PUBLIC HEALTH IN THE 21ST CENTURY

CONTEMPORARY ISSUES IN PUBLIC HEALTH IN NORTH AFRICA AND THE MIDDLE EAST

PUBLIC HEALTH IN THE 21ST CENTURY

Additional books in this series can be found on Nova's website
under the Series tab.

Additional e-books in this series can be found on Nova's website
under the e-book tab.

PUBLIC HEALTH IN THE 21ST CENTURY

CONTEMPORARY ISSUES IN PUBLIC HEALTH IN NORTH AFRICA AND THE MIDDLE EAST

SAMUEL GYASI OBENG
AHMED YOUSSEFAGHA
AND
WASANTHA PARAKRAMA JAYAWARDENE
EDITORS

New York

Copyright © 2014 by Nova Science Publishers, Inc.

All rights reserved. No part of this book may be reproduced, stored in a retrieval system or transmitted in any form or by any means: electronic, electrostatic, magnetic, tape, mechanical photocopying, recording or otherwise without the written permission of the Publisher.

For permission to use material from this book please contact us:
Telephone 631-231-7269; Fax 631-231-8175
Web Site: http://www.novapublishers.com

NOTICE TO THE READER

The Publisher has taken reasonable care in the preparation of this book, but makes no expressed or implied warranty of any kind and assumes no responsibility for any errors or omissions. No liability is assumed for incidental or consequential damages in connection with or arising out of information contained in this book. The Publisher shall not be liable for any special, consequential, or exemplary damages resulting, in whole or in part, from the readers' use of, or reliance upon, this material. Any parts of this book based on government reports are so indicated and copyright is claimed for those parts to the extent applicable to compilations of such works.

Independent verification should be sought for any data, advice or recommendations contained in this book. In addition, no responsibility is assumed by the publisher for any injury and/or damage to persons or property arising from any methods, products, instructions, ideas or otherwise contained in this publication.

This publication is designed to provide accurate and authoritative information with regard to the subject matter covered herein. It is sold with the clear understanding that the Publisher is not engaged in rendering legal or any other professional services. If legal or any other expert assistance is required, the services of a competent person should be sought. FROM A DECLARATION OF PARTICIPANTS JOINTLY ADOPTED BY A COMMITTEE OF THE AMERICAN BAR ASSOCIATION AND A COMMITTEE OF PUBLISHERS.

Additional color graphics may be available in the e-book version of this book.

Library of Congress Cataloging-in-Publication Data

Contemporary issues in public health in North Africa and the Middle East / Editors: Samuel Gyasi Obeng, Ahmed Youssefagha and Wasantha Parakrama Jayawardene (African Studies Program & The School of Public Health, Indiana University, IN, USA).
    pages cm -- (Public health in the 21st century)
  Includes index.
  ISBN: 978-1-63117-933-4 (softcover)
 1. Public health--Africa, North. 2. Public health--Middle East. I. Obeng, Samuel Gyasi, editor. II. Youssefagha, Ahmed, editor. III. Jayawardene, Wasantha Parakrama, editor.
 RA447.N85C66 2014
 362.1096--dc23
                                  2014015858

Published by Nova Science Publishers, Inc. † New York

CONTENTS

Preface		vii
Introduction		ix
	Samuel Gyasi Obeng	
Chapter 1	Characteristics of Diabetes Epidemic in the Arabian Peninsula and other Muslim Countries *Wasantha Jayawardene, Ahmed Youssefagha, Samir Matter and Ammal Mokhtar*	1
Chapter 2	Primary Prevention of Diabetes in North Africa and the Middle East Region: An Ecological Perspective *Ahmed Youssefagha, Chelsea Heaven, Adrienne Luegers, Nancy Morales and Wasantha Jayawardene*	19
Chapter 3	Hepatitis B and C in Refugees from Northeast Africa: The Need for Screening *Ahmed Youssefagha, Wasantha Jayawardene and David Lohrmann*	35
Chapter 4	Prediction of Total Water Requirements for Agriculture in the Arab World under Climate Change *Gamal El Afandi, Samiha Ouda, Fouad Khalil and Sayed Abd El-Hafez*	51

Chapter 5	Role of Infrastructure Development and Prevention in Combat against HIV/AIDS in Africa: Opportunities Being Lost *Wasantha Jayawardene, Ahmed Youssefagha, Susan Middlestadt, David Lohrmann and Mohamed Torabi*	67
Chapter 6	A Comparison of the Egyptian Public's Rankings of Key Public Health and Environmental Issues by Occupation and by Gender *Ahmed Youssefagha, Brian Chen, Nargis Labib, David Lohrmann, Rasha Salama and Nagla ElSherbibi*	89
Editors' Contact Information		109
Index		111

PREFACE

Speakers of Latin of Old put it in a rather poetic way:
Mens sana in corpore sano
A sound mind in a sound body
A healthy mind, they said, in a healthy body!
But have our bodies been healthy?
Our lifestyles have not in any way paved the way for our bodies to be healthy!
We appear to be living on borrowed time
A time we do not own or even know about
We dislike learning about our health
Yet we want to enjoy good health
We taboo talking about our state of mind
Yet we want to stay safe and in a sound mind!
These knowledge-seeking and solution-finding individuals
Have done their best to unearth what is wrong with our bodies
They have investigated what causes our bodies to be diseased and unhealthy
They have educated us on ways of ensuring that our minds are sound!
We better read and act now
Lest we damage mind, body and soul!
We better wake up and take action right away
Lest we cause our extinction from the face of this beautiful land!
We better read and learn
Lest affliction and woes gain permanent abode in our bodies and minds
This is the time!
It is now or never!

Let's read and educate ourselves about our own health!
Let's help the world by staying sound in body and in mind!

INTRODUCTION

Samuel Gyasi Obeng
Indiana University, Woodburn Hall, Bloomington, IN, US

The papers in this volume answer the call by scholars in the fields of Public Health, Community Health, Medicine, Bio-Statistics, and Decision Science, as well as those by political actors, policy experts, and various world bodies dealing with health and safety in North Africa and the Middle East to address the intellectual lacuna left by the dearth of scholarship on contemporary health, environmental and safety issues in the above-mentioned region of the world. In putting together this volume, every attempt was made to invite experts whose scholarships are respected and who have a firsthand knowledge of the region. The topics covered are wide and the depth is unquestionably outstanding. Many a time, especially, this past decade, work on Africa, be it north or Sub-Saharan, has concentrated solely, if not absolutely, on HIV and AIDS to the neglect of equally important ailments bedeviling the continent. Those on the Middle East have not been any different. It is therefore credit-worthy and gratifying that the authors in this volume go beyond this 'norm' and deal with HIV and AIDS and also devote considerable space and effort to synthesize and analyze such important health issues as diabetes, hepatitis and C, as well as water and its associated agricultural and health issues. Even more important and innovative about this volume is the attempt by the authors to examine real and/or actual views of the research populations on environmental and public health issues based on participants' occupation and gender.

Chapter 1 examines the characteristics of the diabetes epidemic in the Arabian Peninsula and in other Muslim countries. Specifically, the authors investigate whether the Islamic religion plays any significant role in determining the main characteristics of diabetes epidemic in Islamic countries worldwide in general, and in the Arabian Peninsula in particular. The authors conducted a Medline search of articles from 1990 to 2009 and identified 91 studies, including 13 from the Arabian region and 13 from non-Arabian Islamic countries. Results indicated that overall, the prevalence of diabetes was relatively higher in the Arabian region (10.5%) compared to rest of the world, while it was considerably lower (6.2%) than rest of the world for impaired glucose tolerance (IGT). The authors discovered further that countries in the Arabian Peninsula had an overall higher prevalence of diabetes, lower prevalence of IGT, and higher prevalence of diabetes among men than in women. There was also a higher prevalence of IGT in women than in men in the Arabian Peninsula compared to other regions of the world. Finally, the authors discovered that prevalence of life-style related risk factors in Islamic countries vary considerably in different regions of the world.

The object of Chapter 2 is a synthesis and analysis of the primary prevention strategies of diabetes in North Africa and the Middle East Region from an ecological perspective. In particular, the authors conducted an ecological analysis to examine the differences in diet and lifestyle between countries in the Middle East and North African (MENA) region identified as having a high, medium, and low prevalence of diabetes based on the regional average. Data sources for the research included the International Diabetes Federation, World Health Organization, and The Food and Agriculture Organization of the United Nations. They discovered that throughout the past few decades, rapid economic development, urbanization, and social and lifestyle changes have contributed to the increase of diabetes prevalence in the MENA region. The authors noted, however, that, to date few analyses have utilized GDP, population, and food security data to investigate differences between countries inside the MENA region plagued by high, medium, and low prevalence of diabetes. They discovered that on average, countries in the high diabetes prevalence group have higher GDP, lower population, and higher meat consumption than countries in the medium and low diabetes prevalence groups. Countries in the medium and low prevalence groups had significant increases in the consumption of kilocalories and fat from 1990-2007, while countries in the high prevalence group did not have any increases over time.

The object of Chapter 3 is an examination of Hepatitis B and C infection in refugees from Northeast Africa and the need for appropriate screening. The authors note that the Middle East and North Africa, regions with high prevalence of hepatitis B and C, are major origins of refugees in the United

States. They note further that the incidence of hepatitis B and C is increasing in refugee populations (in the US despite) despite the fact the overall incidence of hepatitis B is decreasing and that of hepatitis C has almost leveled off during the past decade in the U.S. The authors identify lack of screening and cultural differences between refugees and those of the US as barriers to optimal and efficient health care. The authors argue that it is essential that screenings of the above-mentioned diseases be performed before the refugees' departure from their home countries or immediately after their arrival in the US. In particular, given that hepatitis C is often asymptomatic and can become chronic, the authors call for the screening of viral hepatitis, immunization of HBV, followed with more comprehensive treatment and follow-up of care for refugees positive with the infection in order to decrease the risk of transmission and mortality rates.

The object of Chapter 4 is a development of prediction equations to calculate total water requirements needed to support irrigation in each country in the Arab world in 2025 under the expected 2.0°C increase in temperature. The authors gathered, from the Arabic Center for Dry and Arid Zones Studies, data for actual and future amounts of water that is required for agriculture. Results of a regression of the data for mean annual temperature of 100 years for each of the country on future amounts of water required for agriculture (with the view to developing the equations) showed that by 2025 the demand for irrigation water will increase in all the Arab countries, a situation that will create a problem in allocation of water resources between different sectors. Furthermore, the results showed that the Arab countries could be divided into three groups according to the temperature range. Egypt, Djibouti, Libya, Oman, Somalia, Sudan, and Yemen —countries where the *range* was identified as being less than 2.0 °C — were categorized as Group 1. The authors discovered that by 2025 Egypt would have 57.39% increase in water requirements (the highest percentage increase) whereas the Sudan was expected to have an anticipated 20.89% increase (the lowest percentage increase). Group 2 included Algeria, Tunisia, Mauritania, and Maraca— countries where the temperature range was anticipated to be between 2.0 to 2.6°C. Among the above-mentioned countries, Algeria was expected to have the highest percent increase (24.12%) in water requirements by 2025 whereas Tunisia was expected to have the lowest percentage (10.12%) in the group. Group (3) countries consisted of Bahrain, Iraq, Jordan, Kuwait, Lebanon, Palestine, Qatar, Saudi Arabia, Syria, and United Arab Emirates. The range of temperature in the above-mentioned countries is expected to be higher than 2.6°C. Among countries in this group, it is anticipated that Saudi Arabia would have a 43.14% increase in water requirements by 2025 (the highest percentage increase) whereas Lebanon will have the lowest percentage (12.74%). The authors recommend that in order to conserve water and avoid the wasteful use of water resources it is imperative that the concerned Arab governments use adaptation measures.

The authors, in Chapter 5, note that HIV epidemic is worsening in Africa due to poverty, food insecurity, lower level of education, social injustice, and violence. Their review of 73 studies from five databases confirmed that knowledge levels about the causes and spread of STIs vary widely in Africa. Specifically, whereas some people were well informed about issues related to protection against STIs and therefore sought treatment, others did. The authors also identified a discrepancy between awareness and behavior cognizant of the fact that there existed significant deviation in behaviors even in situations where knowledge levels were high. Given the discrepancy between awareness and behavior, the authors call for a reorientation of sexuality education to include social, interpersonal, and theoretical aspects associated with difficult behavioral choices and behavioral change. In particular, they call for a reorientation of sexuality education composed of addressing gender discrepancies through planned intervention programs, promoting skills such as communicating effectively, refusing to engage in risky behaviors, negotiating use of protection, correctly and consistently using condoms, and seeking medical help. The authors conclude by calling for a number of interventions designed to address the issues related to prevention skills, counseling and testing, and infrastructure development.

In Chapter 6, Youssefagha et al., examine the Egyptian public's opinions on the priorities of public health and environmental health issues in Egypt with the view to exploring the differences in the ranked orders based on participants' occupation and gender. The research, which involved the use of 318 participants and an anonymous self-administrative questionnaire, took place in Al Fayuim, Egypt, from 2009 to 2010. In order to compare the distribution of ranks among the public health and environmental issues, the researchers used a *weighted ranking score system*, and *principal component analysis* to help provide a better confirmation of their results. To help show the relevance of their study in relation to other studies, the authors compared the top ranked public health and environmental issues with those of current World Health Organization reports. Results form their study showed that whereas respondents ranked accident prevention and ground drinking water as the least important public health/environmental concern, maternal health and drinking water were ranked as the highest level of concern. The authors discovered further that whereas there was a significant difference between men and women in their rankings of the public and environmental health issues, only a slight difference between the rankings of health and non-health professional groups was noticed. The difference in ranking by men and women was attributed to the inequality of the social roles performed by men and women. Maternal health and education, disease control, nutrition and environment, and immunization, were the four factors found to explain the wide variation in the rankings. Research participants also identified drinking water as an important issue in need of exploration across the six nation-states in North Africa. Based on the results of their findings, the authors note that in order to make the best strategic policy and planning decisions, it is concomitant that health practitioners and governments survey the opinions from a larger population sample and/or a variety of groups. The authors viewed the non-probability sampling method that they used as a limitation given the fact that it is capable of inhibiting generalization of findings to populations beyond the research participants. To ameliorate this limitation, the authors call for the use of larger surveys with randomized sampling.

In: Contemporary Issues in Public Health
Editors: S.G. Obeng, A. Youssefagha et al.
ISBN: 978-1-63117-933-4
© 2014 Nova Science Publishers, Inc.

Chapter 1

CHARACTERISTICS OF DIABETES EPIDEMIC IN THE ARABIAN PENINSULA AND OTHER MUSLIM COUNTRIES

Wasantha Jayawardene[1], Ahmed Youssefagha[1], Samir Matter[1] and Ammal Mokhtar[2]

[1]Indiana University, Indiana, US
[2]National Research Center, Egypt

ABSTRACT

Six out of the top ten countries in prevalence of diabetes are located in the Arabian region, while another two are Islamic, but they are not located in the Arabian region. This review aimed to investigate whether the Islamic traditions, such as food habits, play a significant role in determining the characteristics of the diabetes epidemic in Islamic countries.

Results indicated that the Arabian region has a higher prevalence of diabetes, although impaired glucose tolerance is less prevalent than in other regions. Obesity is the major risk of diabetes in Islamic countries.

Similarities in life-style risk factors in Islamic countries in different regions of the world indicate that the effect of Islamic traditions, mainly dietary habits, may play a major role in determining characteristics of the diabetes epidemic.

INTRODUCTION

Diabetes is a chronic condition that occurs due to either insulin insufficiency (type-1) or the inability of the body to utilize insulin effectively (type-2). Hyperglycemia and other related disturbances in the metabolism can lead to serious damage of many functional systems, especially the nerves and blood vessels. Most diabetics have type-2 diabetes, many with the disease dormant for many years, often diagnosed only after complications have set in. Complications associated with diabetes are cardiovascular disease (the most common cause of death), diabetic neuropathy (the most common complication), diabetic retinopathy, diabetic nephropathy, diabetic foot disease, which can lead to amputations, and impotence in men. Impaired Glucose Tolerance (IGT) can be defined as a pre-diabetic stage. These patients have a disturbance in glucose metabolism, but they do not fit in with the diagnostic criteria for diabetes. They have an increased probability of being diagnosed with diabetes in the future. Because of its chronic nature and the severity of its complications, diabetes is a costly disease; not only for affected individuals, but also for the economies of countries that have a high incidence.

The following are the risk factors for Type-2 diabetes (American Diabetes Association, 2010):

1. Impaired glucose tolerance (IGT) and/or impaired fasting glucose (IFG)
2. Age > 45
3. Family history of diabetes
4. Overweight or obesity
5. Sedentary lifestyle
6. Low HDL cholesterol or high triglycerides
7. Hypertension
8. Certain racial and ethnic groups (e.g., from US: non-Hispanic Blacks, American Indians, Hispanic/Latino Americans, Asian Americans and Pacific Islanders, and Alaskan Natives)
9. Gestational diabetes, or women who had a baby with birth weight >9 pounds

The World Health Organization (WHO) estimates that the top ten countries, in numbers of sufferers from diabetes, are India, China, US, Indonesia, Japan, Pakistan, Russia, Brazil Italy, and Bangladesh (WHO, 2010).

Of these countries, Indonesia, Pakistan, and Bangladesh are predominantly Islamic countries, although they are not located in the Arabian region.

However, six out of the top ten countries in prevalence of diabetes for ages 20–79 (Table 1) are located in the Arabian region: United Arab Emirates, Saudi Arabia, Bahrain, Kuwait, Oman, and Egypt (International Diabetes Federation, 2008). Therefore, more research is required to investigate the existence of relationships between occurrence of diabetes and characteristics of Islamic religion, such as fasting, entertaining eating-habits, consumption of desserts with high-sugar-content, consumption of food with high-fat-content, and less physical activity or sports for women.

Research is also required to investigate any possible genetic predisposition to the occurrence of diabetes in Arabian populations. In addition, primary prevention should be emphasized in these countries, but particularly in the poorer regions where resources are limited.

Healthy diet and regular physical activity have a great impact by reducing or delaying the occurrence of diabetes.

It is evident that among countries with higher prevalence of diabetes, a significantly higher proportion consists of Islamic countries. The purpose of this study is performing a systematic review of previous research to investigate whether the Islamic religion plays a role in determining main characteristics of diabetes epidemic in Islamic countries worldwide.

Table 1. Top Ten Countries in Prevalence of Diabetes in the 20 – 79 Age Group

Year 2007		Year 2025	
Country	Prevalence (%)	Country	Prevalence (%)
Nauru	30.7	Nauru	32.3
UAE	19.5	UEA	21.9
Saudi Arabia	16.7	Saudi Arabia	18.4
Bahrain	15.2	Bahrain	17.0
Kuwait	14.4	Kuwait	16.4
Oman	13.1	Tonga	15.2
Tonga	12.9	Oman	14.7
Mauritius	11.1	Mauritius	13.4
Egypt	11	Egypt	13.4
Mexico	10.6	Mexico	12.4

UAE: United Arab Emirates.
Source: International Diabetes Federation, 2008.

RESEARCH DESIGN AND METHODS

A Medline search of articles from 1990 to 2009 was conducted. In the initial phase of the search, 115 studies were found to have, as a main objective, the determination of the prevalence and risk factors of diabetes/IGT. In the next phase of selection, 91 studies comprising 57 countries were chosen, as they were compatible with all predetermined criteria for this review:

1. The selected study was conducted during the period 1990 through 2009.
2. The study incorporated a cross-sectional descriptive or cross-sectional analytical study design.
3. The age range included, but was not limited to persons older than 18 years of age.
4. The study sample was not a subset of a general population that was diagnosed with another disease.
5. A sample size of no less than 150 respondents with no upper margin.
6. Diagnosis of diabetes was based on one or more of following measures:
    a. WHO (World Health Association) criteria corresponding to the year of study
    b. ADA (American Diabetes Association) criteria corresponding to the year of study
    c. OGTT (Oral Glucose Tolerance Test)
    d. FBG (Fasting Blood Glucose)
    e. Self-report with confirmed diagnosis

The prevalence of diabetes/IGT and significance of risk factors were documented and analyzed with the SAS statistical program.

The average prevalence of diabetes and IGT for each study was estimated wherever a range of prevalence was provided.

The following parameters were estimated: gender-based prevalence of diabetes and IGT for Arabian and Islamic countries, and significance of eight leading risk factors (ADA, 2010) for diabetes in those countries compared to rest of the world.

RESULTS

Out of a total of 91 studies, 13 are from the Arabian (Middle-Eastern) region, while 26 represent Islamic countries predominantly with an Islamic culture. The sample sizes within the 91 studies ranges from 151 to 47151. The age of participants is ranging from 1 to 99 years old. Many studies have used more than one diagnostic criterion to detect cases of diabetes and IGT: 77% of studies utilized FBG, 68% used OGTT, 41% used WHO criteria, 12% used ADA criteria, and only 8% utilized self-report with confirmed diagnosis.

Overall prevalence of diabetes (Figure 1) is relatively higher in the Arabian region (10.5%) compared to rest of the world (9.3%), but it is considerably lower (6.2%) than rest of the world (10.3%) for IGT. In Islamic countries, overall prevalence is 9.1% for diabetes and 9.5% for IGT, which do not differ much from rest of the world (9.6% and 10.3%, respectively).

In Arabian countries and Islamic countries, men have a higher prevalence of diabetes compared to women (10.7% vs. 9.5% and 9.4% vs. 8.3%, respectively), while men have lower prevalence of IGT compared to women (5.0% vs. 7.2% and 7.5% vs. 10.0%, respectively).

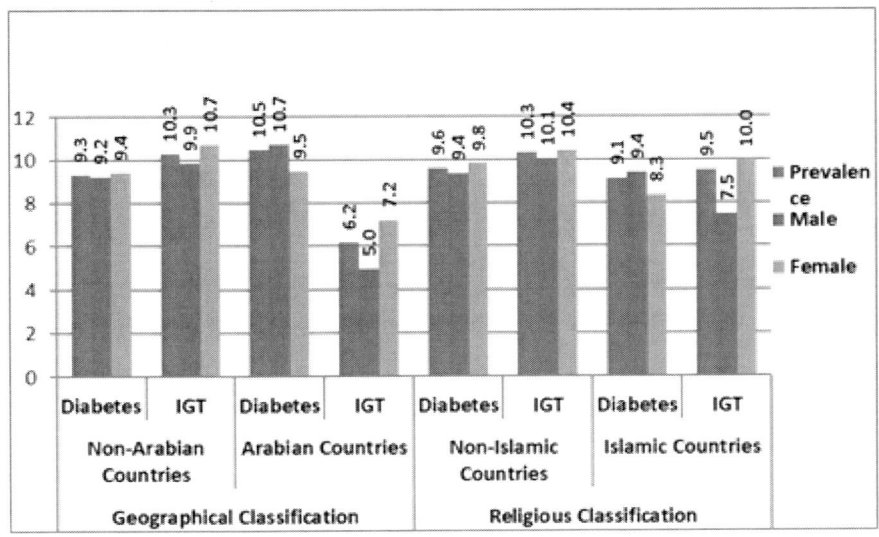

Figure 1. Prevalence of Diabetes and IGT by Gender, according to Geographical and Religious Classifications.

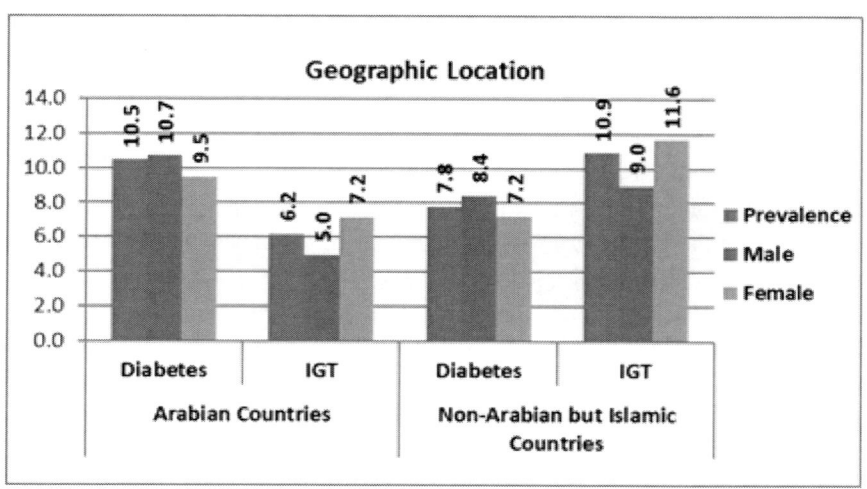

Figure 2. Comparison between Islamic Countries by Geographic Location.

In comparison between Islamic countries by geographic location (Figure 2), it is revealed that diabetes has a considerably higher prevalence in Arabian countries, compared to non-Arabian Islamic countries (10.5% vs. 7.8%), and in contrary, IGT has a considerably lower prevalence in Arabian countries, compared to non-Arabian Islamic countries (6.2% vs. 10.9%).

In Arabian countries, higher prevalence of diabetes compared to non-Arabian Islamic countries is observed in men (10.7% vs. 8.4%) and also in women (9.5% vs. 7.2%).

However, in Arabian countries, lower prevalence of IGT compared to non-Arabian Islamic countries is observed in men (5.0% vs. 9.0%) and also in women (7.2% vs. 11.6%). Older age, obesity, and family history of diabetes are statistically significant ($p < 0.05$) in their association with diabetes in Arabian countries and in Islamic countries compared to rest of the world (Table 2 and 3). Urban area of residence is statistically significant ($p < 0.05$) in its association with diabetes in Islamic countries compared to rest of the world (Table 2). There is no significant difference between these two groups of countries and rest of the world in relation to other risk factors for diabetes. In comparison between Islamic countries by geographic location, it is revealed that the association between central obesity (waist to hip ratio) and diabetes in Non-Arabian Islamic countries is statistically significant when compared to that of Arabian countries.

There is no significant difference between these two groups of countries in relation to other risk factors for diabetes.

Table 2. Prevalence of Diabetes by Age and Area of Residence in Arabian Countries and Islamic Countries Compared with the Rest of the World

Classification	Sub-Category	Age			Area of Residence		
		Yes	No	P-Value	Urban	Rural	P-Value
Geographical	Arabian Countries	85%	15%	0.03	38%	0%	0.44
	Non-Arabian Countries	53%	47%		23%	3%	
By Religion	Islamic Countries	85%	15%	0.00	42%	0%	0.04
	Non-Islamic Countries	46%	54%		18%	3%	

Table 3. Prevalence of Two Selected Predictors of Diabetes (Family History and Obesity) in Arabian Countries and in Islamic Countries, Compared with the Rest of the World

Classification	Sub-Category	Family History			Obesity		
		Yes	No	P-Value	Yes	No	P-Value
Geographical	Arabian Countries	69%	31%	0.03	92%	8%	0.03
	Non-Arabian Countries	37%	63%		62%	38%	
By Religion	Islamic Countries	62%	38%	0.02	88%	12%	0.00
	Non-Islamic Countries	34%	66%		57%	43%	

DISCUSSION

Although the sample size of 91 studies is ranging from 151 to 47151, more than 90% of studies utilized a sample over 500. Therefore, the standard error of the reviewed findings should be relatively low.

Although the age of the participants is ranging from 1 to 99 years old, more than 90% of studies recruited persons older than 18 years of age.

Therefore, the ability to generalize the findings of this review is more applicable to persons older than 18 years worldwide.

A majority of the studies used more than one diagnostic criterion to detect cases of diabetes and IGT.

WHO standards are utilized almost 3.5 times more often compared to ADA standards, probably due to feasibility. Despite the existence of accepted diagnostic standards, such as WHO and ADA criteria, many studies utilized FBG and OGTT alone for detection of cases. Feasibility may be the main factor for non-adherence to a standard diagnostic criterion. All eight studies that used self-reporting alone are from developed countries.

A high prevalence is recorded in the Arabian region compared to rest of the world, which is an expected finding because there are many countries with higher prevalence of diabetes in that region. Interestingly, it has a lower prevalence of IGT, documenting an inverse relationship between the ratio of IGT/diabetes and diabetes prevalence. In addition, Arabian men have a higher prevalence of diabetes compared to women, but this difference is inversed in relation to IGT. In contrast to rest of the world, the Arabian region has a higher prevalence of diabetes than IGT. A similar pattern is also observed in some studies conducted on minority ethnic groups in Americas.

The aforementioned findings are consistent with the hypothesis that those populations with very high rates of diabetes appear to have progressed past the pre-diabetes stages in the natural history of this metabolic disorder (Yu and Zinman, 2007). Non-Arabian Islamic countries, compared to Arabian countries, have a lower prevalence of diabetes, but a higher prevalence of IGT.

Both men and women in non-Arabian Islamic countries have a lower prevalence of diabetes and a higher prevalence of IGT, when compared to Arabian men and women, respectively. In this regard, non-Arabian Islamic countries share more similarities with non-Islamic countries worldwide, but not with Arabian countries.

In an analysis of Arabian countries with rest of the world, statistically significant differences are found between older age, obesity, and family history of diabetes with a prevalence of diabetes. A similar pattern is found in Islamic countries versus other countries in the world in relation to the same risk factors. In an analysis of Islamic countries versus the rest of the world, a statistically significant difference is found between areas of residence with diabetes, which is not observed in the analysis of Arabian countries versus rest of the world. It is observed that the association between central obesity (waist to hip ratio) and diabetes in non-Arabian Islamic countries is statistically significant when compared to that of Arabian countries. In Arabian countries, central obesity is not specifically identified as an important risk factor for diabetes, although obesity is identified as significant.

There is no significant difference between Arabian countries and non-Arabian Islamic countries in relation to other risk factors for diabetes.

Therefore, the Arabian region has specific characteristics in its epidemic of diabetes, because it has an overall higher prevalence of diabetes, an overall lower prevalence of IGT, a higher prevalence of diabetes among men than in women, and a higher prevalence of IGT in women than in men, compared to other regions of the world. This also indicates a possible increase of prevalence of diabetes in women in the future compared to men.

In addition, obesity, older age, and family history of diabetes are common risk factors for all Islamic countries, both Arabian and non-Arabian.

Only one of these risk factors, obesity, can be considered as life-style related or modifiable. Older age and family history are not life-style-related risk factors, and therefore, non-modifiable. A lack of similarities in relation to life-style related risk factors in Islamic countries indicates that the effect of Islamic religion and culture plays a minor role in determining characteristics of epidemic of diabetes.

CONCLUSION

The Arabian world has an overall higher prevalence of diabetes; in addition, the region has an overall lower prevalence of IGT. Compared to other regions of the world, diabetes is prevalent among men than in women and the prevalence of IGT is higher in women than in men. These results are consistent with the hypothesis that those populations with very high rates of diabetes appear to have progressed past the pre-diabetes stages in the natural history of this metabolic disorder.

More research is required to investigate the existence of relationships between the occurrence of diabetes and characteristics of the Islamic religion, such as fasting, entertaining eating-habits, consumption of desserts with high sugar content, consumption of food with high fat content, and less physical activity or sports for women, apart from possible genetic predispositions to the occurrence of diabetes in Arabian populations.

REFERENCES

Abdella, N., Al Arouj, M., Al Nakhi, A., Al Assoussi, A., and Moussa, M. (1998). Non-insulin-dependent diabetes in Kuwait: Prevalence rates and associated risk factors. *Diabetes Res. Clin. Pract.*, 42(3), 187-196.

Abdul-Rahim, H. F., Husseini, A., Giacaman, R., Jervell, J., and Bjertness, E. (2001). Diabetes mellitus in an urban Palestinian population: Prevalence and associated factors. *East Mediterr. Health J.*, 7(1-2), 67-78.

Abu Sayeed, M., Ali, L., Hussain, M. Z., Rumi, M. A., Banu, A., and Azad Khan, A. K. (1997). Effect of socioeconomic risk factors on the difference in prevalence of diabetes between rural and urban populations in Bangladesh. *Diabetes Care*, 20(4), 551-555.

Aekplakorn, W., R. P. Stolk, B. Neal, P. Suriyawongpaisal, V. Chongsuvivatwong, and S. Cheepudomwit. (2003). The prevalence and management of diabetes in Thai adults: The international collaborative study of cardiovascular disease in Asia. *Diabetes Care*, 26(10), 2758-2763.

Ajay, V. S., Prabhakaran, D., Jeemon, P., Thankappan, K. R., Mohan, V., and Ramakrishnan, L. (2008). Prevalence and determinants of diabetes mellitus in the Indian industrial population. *Diabet. Med.*, 25(10), 1187-1194.

Ajlouni, K., Khader, Y. S., Batieha, A., Ajlouni, H., and El-Khateeb, M. (2008). An increase in prevalence Of diabetes mellitus in Jordan over 10 years. *J. Diabetes Complications*, 22(5): 317-324.

Al-Moosa, S., Allin, S., Jemiai, N., Al-Lawati, J., and Mossialos, E. (2006). Diabetes and urbanization in the Omani population: An analysis of national survey data. *Popul. Health Metr.*, 4(5) doi:10.1186/1478-7954-4-5.

Al-Nuaim, A. R. (1997). Prevalence of glucose intolerance in urban and rural communities in Saudi Arabia. *Diabet. Med.*, 14(7), 595-602.

American Diabetes Association. (2010) *Diabetes Basics: Your Risk*. Available from: http://www.diabetes.org Accessed on 07/12/2011.

Anders, R. L., Olson, T., Wiebe, J., Bean, N. H., DiGregorio, R., and Guillermina, M. (2008). Diabetes prevalence and treatment adherence in residents living in a colonia located on the West Texas, US/Mexico border. *Nurs. Health Sci.*, 10(3), 195-202.

Aspray, T. J., Mugusi, F., Rashid, S., Whiting, D., Edwards, R., and Alberti, K. G. (2000). Rural and urban differences in diabetes prevalence in Tanzania: The role of obesity, physical inactivity, and urban living. *Trans. R. Soc. Trop. Med. Hyg.*, 94(6), 637-644.

Baldé, N. M., Diallo, I., Baldé, M. D., Barry, I. S., Kaba, L., and Diallo, M. M. (2007). Diabetes and impaired fasting glucose in rural and urban populations in Futa Jallon (Guinea): Prevalence and associated risk factors. *Diabetes Metab.*, 33(2), 114-120.

Baltazar, J. C., Ancheta, C. A., Aban, I. B., Fernando, R. E., and Baquilod, M. M. (2004). Prevalence and correlates of diabetes mellitus and impaired glucose tolerance among adults in Luzon, Philippines. *Diabetes Res. Clin. Pract.*, 64(2), 107-15.

Bener, A., Zirie, M., Janahi, I. M., Al-Hamaq, A. O., Musallam, M., and Wareham, N. J. (2009). Prevalence of diagnosed and undiagnosed diabetes mellitus and its risk factors in a population-based study of Qatar. *Diabetes Res. Clin. Pract.*, 84(1), 99-106.

Boronat, M., Varillas, V. F., Saavedra, P., Suárez, V., Bosch, E., and Carrillo, A. (2006). Diabetes mellitus and impaired glucose regulation in the Canary Islands (Spain): Prevalence and associated factors in the adult population of Telde, Gran Canaria. *Diabet. Med.,* 23(2), 148-155.

Bouguerra, R., Alberti, H., Salem, L. B., Rayana, C. B., Atti, J. E., and Gaigi, S. (2007). The global diabetes pandemic: The Tunisian experience. *Eur. J. Clin. Nutri.*, 2, 160-165.

Carter, E. A., MacCluer, J. W., Dyke, B., Howard, B. V., Devereux, R. B., and Ebbesson, S. O. (2006). Diabetes mellitus and impaired fasting glucose in Alaska Eskimos: The genetics of coronary artery disease in Alaska Natives (GOCADAN) stud. *Diabetologia*, 49(1), 29-35.

Chang, C., Lu, F., Yang, Y. C., Wu, J. S., Wu, T. J., and Chen, M. S. (2000). Epidemiologic study of type 2 diabetes in Taiwan. *Diabetes Res. Clin. Pract.*, 50(2), S49-59.

Christensen, D. L., Friis, H., Mwaniki, D. L., Kilonzo, B., Tetens, I., and Boit, M. K. (2009). Prevalence of glucose intolerance and associated risk factors in rural and urban populations of different ethnic groups in Kenya. *Diabetes Res. Clin. Pract.*, 84(3), 303-310.

Colagiuri, S., Colagiuri, R., Na'ati, S., Muimuiheata, S., Hussain, Z., and Palu, T. (2002). The prevalence of diabetes in the Kingdom of Tonga. *Diabetes Care*, 25(8), 1378-83.

Collins, V. R., Dowse, G. K., Toelupe, P. M., Imo, T. T., Aloaina, F. L., and Spark, R. A. (1994). Increasing prevalence of NIDDM in the Pacific island population of Western Samoa over a 13-Year period. *Diabetes Care*, 17(4), 288-96.

Danaei, G., Friedman, A. B., Oza, S., Murray, C. J., and Ezzati, M. (2009). Diabetes prevalence and diagnosis in US states: Analysis of health surveys. *Popul. Health Metr.*, 25(7), 16.

Delisle, H. F. and Ekoé, J. M. 1993. Prevalence of non-insulin-dependent diabetes mellitus and impaired glucose tolerance in two Algonquin communities in Quebec. *CMAJ*, 148(1), 41-47.

Dong, Y., Gao, W., Nan, H., Yu, H., Li, F., and Duan, W. (2005). Prevalence of type 2 diabetes in urban and rural Chinese populations in Qingdao, China. *Diabet. Med.*, 22(10), 1427-1433.

Duc Son, L. N., Kusama, K., Hung, N. T., Loan, T. T., Chuyen, N. V., and Kunii, D. (2004). Prevalence and risk factors for diabetes in Ho Chi Minh City, Vietnam. *Diabet. Med.*, 21(4), 371-376.

Ebbesson, S. O., Schraer, C. D., Risica, P. M., Adler, A. I., Ebbesson, L., and Mayer, A. M. (1998). Diabetes and impaired glucose tolerance in three Alaskan Eskimo populations: The Alaska-Siberia project. *Diabetes Care*, 21(4), 563-569.

Elbagir, M. N., Eltom, M. A., Elmahadi, E. M., Kadam, I. M., and Berne, C. (1996). A population-based study of the prevalence of diabetes and impaired glucose tolerance in adults in Northern Sudan. *Diabetes Care*, 19 (10), 1126-1128.

Elbagir, M. N., Eltom, M. A., Elmahadi, E. M., Kadam, I. M., and Berne, C. (1998). A high prevalence of diabetes mellitus and impaired glucose tolerance in the Danagla community in Northern Sudan. *Diabet. Med.*, 15 (2), 164-169.

Escobedo, J., Buitrón, L. V., Velasco, M. F., Ramírez, J. C., Hernández, R., and Macchia, A. (2009). High prevalence of diabetes and impaired fasting glucose in urban Latin America: The CARMELA study. *Diabet. Med.*, 26 (9), 864-871.

Escolar Pujolar, A. (2009). Social determinants vs. lifestyle in type 2 diabetes mellitus in Andalusia (Spain): Difficulty in making ends meet or obesity? *Gac. Sanit.*, 23(5), 427-432.

Ford, E. S., Mokdad, A. H., Giles, W. H., Galuska, D. A., and Serdula, M. K. (2005). Geographic variation in the prevalence of obesity, diabetes, and obesity-related behaviors. *Obes. Res.*, 13(1), 118-122.

Gao, W. G., Dong, Y. H., Pang, Z. C., Nan, H. R., Zhang, L., and Wang, S. J. (2009). Increasing trend in the prevalence of type 2 diabetes and pre-diabetes in the Chinese rural and urban population in Qingdao, China. *Diabet. Med.*, 26(12), 1220-1227.

Glümer, C., Jørgensen, T. and Borch-Johnsen, K. (2003). Prevalences of diabetes and impaired glucose regulation in a Danish population: The Inter-99 study. *Diabetes Care*, 26(8), 2335-2340.

Gordon, D. L., Cook, C. B., Scheer, W. D., Oalmann, M., Boudreau, D. A., and Borne, D. (1999). Diabetes and obesity in the Louisiana Coushatta Indians. *Ethn. Dis.*, 9(1), 48-58.

Gourdy, P., Ruidavets, J. B., Ferrieres, J., Ducimetiere, P., Amouyel, P., and Arveiler, D. (2001). Prevalence of type 2 diabetes and impaired fasting glucose in the middle-aged population of three French regions: The MONICA study, 1995-97. *Diabetes Metab.*, 27(3), 347-358.

Hadaegh, F., Bozorgmanesh, M. R., Ghasemi, A., Harati, H., Saadat, N., and Azizi, F. (2008). High prevalence of undiagnosed diabetes and abnormal glucose tolerance in the Iranian urban population: Tehran lipid and glucose study. *BMC Public Health*, 8, 176.

Herman, W. H., Ali, M. A., Aubert, R. E., Engelgau, M. M., Kenny, S. J., and Gunter, E. W. (1995). Diabetes mellitus in Egypt: Risk factors and prevalence. *Diabet. Med.*, 12(12), 1126-1131.

Hussain, A., Rahim, M. A., Azad Khan, A. K., Ali, S. M., and Vaaler, S. (2005). Type 2 diabetes in rural and urban population: Diverse prevalence and associated risk factors in Bangladesh. *Diabet. Med.*, 22(7), 931-936.

International Diabetes Federation. (2008). *Diabetes Atlas: The Global Burden.* Available from http://www.idf.org/. Accessed on 07/13/2011.

Jimenez, J. T., Palacios, M., Cañete, F., Barriocanal, L. A., Medina, U., and Figueredo, R. (1998). Prevalence of diabetes mellitus and associated cardiovascular risk factors in an adult urban population in Paraguay. *Diabet. Med.*, 15(4), 334-338.

Jorgensen, M. E., Bjeregaard, P. and Borch-Johnsen, K. (2002). Diabetes and impaired glucose tolerance among the Inuit population of Greenland. *Diabetes Care*, 25(10), 1766-1771.

Kadiki, O. A. and Roaeid, R. B. (2001). Prevalence of diabetes mellitus and impaired glucose tolerance in Benghazi Libya. *Diabetes Metab.*, 27(6), 647-654.

Kasiam, L. O., Longo-Mbenza, B., Nge, O. A., Kangola, K. N., Mbungu, F. S., and Milongo, D. G. (2009). Classification and dramatic epidemic of diabetes mellitus in Kinshasa Hinterland: The prominent role of type 2 diabetes and lifestyle changes among Africans. *Niger. J. Med.*, 18(3), 311-320.

Katulanda, P., Constantine, G. R., Mahesh, J. G., Sheriff, R., Seneviratne, R. D., and Wijeratne, S. (2008). Prevalence and projections of diabetes and pre-diabetes in adults in Sri Lanka: Sri Lanka diabetes, cardiovascular study (SLDCS). *Diabet. Med.* 25(9), 1062-1069.

Kim, S. G., Yang, S. W., Jang, A. S., Seo, J. P., Han, S. W., and Yeom, C. H. (2002). Prevalence of diabetes mellitus in the elderly of Namwon County, South Korea. *Korean J. Intern. Med.*, 17(3), 180-190.

King, H., Abdullaev, B., Djumaeva, S., Nikitin, V., Ashworth, L., and Dobo, M. G. (1998). Glucose intolerance and associated factors in the Fergana Valley, Uzbekistan. *Diabet. Med.*, 15(12), 1052-1062.

Kiss, C., Poór, G., Donáth, J., Gergely, P., Paksy, A., and Zajkás, G. (2003). Prevalence of obesity in an elderly Hungarian population. *Eur. J. Epidemiol.*, 18(7), 653-657.

Lee, E. T., Howard, B. V., Savage, P. J., Cowan, L. D., Fabsitz, R. R., and Oopik, A. J. (1995). Diabetes and impaired glucose tolerance in three American Indian populations aged 45-74 years: The Strong Heart Study. *Diabetes Care*, 18(5), 599-610.

Lerman, I. G., Villa, A. R., Martinez, C. L., Cervantes Turrubiatez, L., Aguilar Salinas, C. A., and Wong, B. (1998). The prevalence of diabetes and associated coronary risk factors in urban and rural older Mexican populations. *J. Am. Geriatr. Soc.*, 46(11), 1387-1395.

Li, R., Lu, W., Jia, W. P., Li, Y. Y., Shi, L., and Liu, M. X. (2006). Cross-sectional investigation of prevalence of type 2 diabetes in Shanghai. *Zhonghua Yi Xue Za Zhi*, 86(24), 1675-1680.

Lionis, C. D., Sasarolis, S. M., Koutis, A. D., Antonakis, N. A., Benos, A., and Papavasiliou, S. (1996). Measuring the prevalence of diabetes mellitus in a Greek primary health care district. *Fam. Pract.*, 13(1), 18-21.

Liu, P., Li, Y. and Yu, H. (1999). Relationship between diabetes mellitus, impaired glucose tolerance and age, menopause, pregnancy: A survey of 5153 women in Shenzhen. *China Med. J. (Engl.)*, 112(7), 612-614.

Łopatyński, J., Mardarowicz, G. and Szcześniak, G. (2003). A comparative evaluation of waist circumference, waist-to-hip ratio, waist-to-height ratio, and body mass index as indicators of impaired glucose tolerance and as risk factors for type 2 diabetes mellitus. *Ann. Univ. Mariae Curie Sklodowska Med.*, 58(1), 413-419.

Mbanya, J. C., Ngogang, J., Salah, J. N., Minkoulou, E., and Balkau, B. (1997). Prevalence of NIDDM and impaired glucose tolerance in a rural and an urban population in Cameroon. *Diabetologia*, 40(7), 824-829.

McDonald, M., Hertz, R. P., Unger, A. N., and Lustik, M. B. (2009). Prevalence, awareness, and management of hypertension, dyslipidemia, and diabetes among United States adults aged 65 and older. *J. Gerontol. A Biol. Sci. Med. Sci.*, 64(2), 256-263.

Melidonis, A. M., Tournis, S. M., Kompoti, M. K., Lentzas, I. L., Roussou, V. R., and Iraklianou, S. L. (2006). Increased prevalence of diabetes mellitus in a rural Greek population. *Rural Remote Health*, 6(1), 534.

Menon, V. U., Kumar, K. V., Gilchrist, A., Sugathan, T. N., Sundaram, K. R., and Nair, V. (2006). Prevalence of known and undetected diabetes and associated risk factors in central Kerala-ADEPS. *Diabetes Res. Clin. Pract.*, 74(3), 289-294.

Mihardja, L., Manz, H. S., Ghani, L., and Soegondo, S. (2009). Prevalence and determinants of diabetes mellitus and impaired glucose tolerance in Indonesia: A part of basic healthrResearch/riskesdas. *Acta Med. Indones.*, 41(4), 169-174.

Misra, A., Pandey, R. M., Devi, J. R., Sharma, R., Vikram, N. K., and Khanna, N. (2001). High prevalence of diabetes, obesity, and dyslipidaemia in urban slum population in Northern India. *Int. J. Obes. Relat. Metab. Disord.*, 25(11), 1722-1729.

Mohan, V., Mathur, P., Deepa, R., Deepa, M., Shukla, D. K., and Menon, G. R. (2008). Urban rural differences in prevalence of self-reported diabetes in India: The WHO-ICMR Indian NCD risk factor surveillance. *Diabetes Res. Clin. Pract.*, 80(1), 159-168.

Motala, A. A., Esterhuizen, T., Gouws, E., Pirie, F. J., and Omar, M. A. (2008). Diabetes and other disorders of glycemia in a rural South African community: Prevalence and associated risk factors. *Diabetes Care*, 31(9), 1783-1788.

Mozaffarian, D., Kamineni, A., Carnethon, M, Djoussé, L., Mukamal, K. J., and Siscovick, D. (2009). Lifestyle risk factors and new-onset diabetes mellitus in older adults: The cardiovascular health study. *Arch. Intern. Med.*, 169(8), 798-807.

Mykkänen, L., Laakso, M., Uusitupa, M., and Pyörälä, K. (1990). Prevalence of diabetes and impaired glucose tolerance in elderly subjects and their association with obesity and family history of diabetes. *Diabetes Care*, 13 (11), 1099-1105.

Ning, F., Pang, Z. C., Dong, Y. H., Gao, W. G., Nan, H. R., and Wang, S. J. (2009). Risk factors associated with the dramatic increase in the prevalence of diabetes in the adult Chinese population in Qingdao, China. *Diabet. Med.*, 26(9), 855-863.

Nthangeni, G., Steyn, N. P., Alberts, M., Steyn, K, Levitt, N. S., and Laubscher, R. (2002). Dietary intake and barriers to dietary compliance in Black type 2 diabetic patients attending primary health-care services. *Public Health Nutr.*, 5(2), 329-338.

Oza-Frank, R. and Narayan, K. M. (2010). Overweight and diabetes prevalence among US immigrants. *Am. J. Public Health,* 100(4): 661–668.

Papazoglou, N., Manes, C., Chatzimitrofanous, P., Papadeli, E., Tzounas, K., and Scaragas, G. (1995). Epidemiology of diabetes mellitus in the elderly in Northern Greece: A population study. *Diabet. Med.*, 12(5), 397-400.

Pérez-Bravo, F., Carrasco, E., Santos, J. L., Calvillán, M., Larenas, G., and Albala, C. (2001). Prevalence of type 2 diabetes and obesity in rural Mapuche population from Chile. *Nutrition*, 17(3), 236-238.

Rafique, G. and Khuwaja, A. K. (2003). Diabetes and hypertension: Public awareness and lifestyle: Findings of a health mela. *J. Coll. Physicians Surg. Pak.*, 13(12), 679-683.

Ramachandran, A., Snehalatha, C. and Vijay, V. (2002). Temporal changes in prevalence of type 2 diabetes and impaired glucose tolerance in urban Southern India. *Diabetes Res. Clin. Pract.*, 58(1), 55-60.

Ramachandran, A., Snehalatha, C., Shyamala, P., Vijay, V., and Viswanathan, M. (1994). High prevalence of NIDDM and IGT in an elderly South Indian population with low rates of obesity. *Diabetes Care*, 17(10), 1190-1192.

Ramaiya, K. L., Swai, A. B., McLarty, D. G., and Alberti, K. G. (1991). Impaired glucose tolerance and diabetes mellitus in Hindu Indian immigrants in Dar Es Salaam. *Diabet. Med.*, 8(8), 738-744.

Rguibi, M. and Belahsen, R. (2006). Prevalence and associated risk factors of undiagnosed diabetes among adult Moroccan Sahraoui women. *Public Health Nutr.*, 9(6), 722-727.

Rodriguez, B. L., Curb, J. D., Burchfiel, C. M., Huang, B., Sharp, D. S., and Lu, G. Y. (1996). Impaired glucose tolerance, diabetes, and cardiovascular disease risk factor profiles in the elderly: The Honolulu heart Pprogram. *Diabetes Care*, 19(6), 587-590.

Saadi, H., Carruthers, S. G., Nagelkerke, N., Al-Maskari, F., Afandi, B., and Reed, R. (2007). Prevalence of diabetes mellitus and its complications in a population-based sample in Al Ain, United Arab Emirates. *Diabetes Res. Clin. Pract.*, 78(3), 369-377.

Satman, I., Yilmaz, T., Sengül, A., Salman, S., Salman, F., and Uygur, S. (2002). Population-based study of diabetes and risk characteristics in Turkey: Results of the Turkish diabetes epidemiology study (TURDEP). *Diabetes Care*, 25(9), 1551-1556.

Sayeed, M. A., Mahtab, H., Akter Khanam, P., Abdul Latif, Z., Keramat Ali, S. M., and Banu, A. (2003). Diabetes and impaired fasting glycemia in a rural population of Bangladesh. *Diabetes Care*, 26(4), 1034-1039.

Sekikawa, A., Eguchi, H., Tominaga, M., Igarashi, K., Abe, T., and Manaka, H. (2000). Prevalence of type 2 diabetes mellitus and impaired glucose tolerance in a rural area of Japan: The Funagata diabetes study. *J. Diabetes Complications*, 14(2), 78-83.

Shera, A. S., Jawad, F. and Maqsood, A. (2007). Prevalence of diabetes in Pakistan. *Diabetes Res. Clin. Pract.*, 76(2), 219-222.

Shera, A. S., Rafique, G., Khawaja, I. A., Baqai, S., and King, H. (1999). Pakistan national diabetes survey: Prevalence of glucose intolerance and associated factors in Baluchistan Province. *Diabetes Res. Clin. Pract.*, 44 (1), 49-58.

Shi, H. L., Fang, J. C. and Zhu, X. X. (1998). Prevalence of diabetes mellitus and associated risk factors in an adult urban population in Shanghai. *Diabetes Metab.*, 24(6), 539-542.

Shrestha, U. K., Singh, D. L. and Bhattarai, M. D. (2006). The prevalence of hypertension and diabetes defined by fasting and 2-H plasma glucose criteria in urban Nepal. *Diabet. Med.*, 23(10), 1130-1135.

Smith, S. M., Holohan, J., McAuliffe, A., and Firth, R. G. (2003). Irish diabetes detection programme in general practice. *Diabet. Med.*, 20(9), 717-722.

Snehalatha, C., Ramchandran, A., Kapur, A., and Vijay, V. (2003). Age-specific prevalence and risk associations for impaired glucose tolerance in urban Southern Indian population. *J. Assoc. Physicians India*, 51, 766-769.

Suvd, J., Gerel, B., Otgooloi, H., Purevsuren, D., Zolzaya, H., and Roglic, G. (2002). Glucose intolerance and associated factors in Mongolia: Results of a national survey. *Diabet. Med.*, 19(6), 502-508.

Szurkowska, M., Szafraniec, K., Gilis-Januszewska, A., Pach, D., Krzentowska, A., and Szybiński, Z. (2006). Prevalence of the glucose metabolism disturbances in screening of adult inhabitants of Krakow. *Przegl. Lek.*, 63(9), 728-732.

Szybiński, Z. (2001). Polish multicenter study on diabetes epidemiology (PMSDE)-1998-2000. *Pol. Arch. Med. Wewn.*, 106(3), 751-758.

Taylor, R., Jalaludin, B., Levy, S., Montaville, B., Gee, K., and Sladden, T. (1991). Prevalence of diabetes, hypertension, and obesity at different levels of urbanisation in Vanuatu. *Med. J. Aust.*, 155(2), 86-90.

Thomas, M. C., Walker, M. K., Emberson, J. R., Thomson, A. G., Lawlor, D. A., and Ebrahim, S. (2005). Prevalence of undiagnosed type 2 diabetes and impaired fasting glucose in older British men and women. *Diabet. Med.*, 22(6), 789-793.

Torquato, M. T., Montenegro Jr, R. M., Viana, L. A., de Souza, R. A., Lanna, C. M., and Lucas, J. C. (2003). Prevalence of diabetes mellitus and impaired glucose tolerance in the urban population aged 30-69 years in Ribeirão Preto (São Paulo), Brazil. *Sao Paulo Med. J.*, 121(6), 224-230.

Vozár, J. (2001). The prevalence of undiagnosed type 2 diabetes mellitus in consulting rooms of general practitioners. *Vnitr. Lek.*, 47(3), 140-145.

Wijewardene, K., Mohideen, M. R., Mendis, S., Fernando, D. S., Kulathilaka, T., and Weerasekara, D. (2005). Prevalence of hypertension, diabetes, and obesity: Baseline findings of a population based survey in four provinces in Sri Lanka. *Ceylon Med. J.*, 50(2), 62-70.

World Health Organization. *Diabetes Program: Facts and Figures about Diabetes (2010)*. Available from www.who.org Accessed on 07/16/2011.

Yu, C. H. Y. and Zinman, B. (2007). Type 2 diabetes and impaired glucose tolerance in aboriginal populations: A global perspective. *Diabetes Res. Clin. Prac.*, 78(2), 159-170.

Zargar, A. H., Khan, A. K., Masoodi, S. R., Laway, B. A., Wani, A. I., and Bashir, M. I. (2000). Prevalence of type 2 diabetes mellitus and impaired glucose tolerance in the Kashmir Valley of the Indian subcontinent. *Diabetes Res. Clin. Pract.*, 47(2), 135-146.

Chapter 2

PRIMARY PREVENTION OF DIABETES IN NORTH AFRICA AND THE MIDDLE EAST REGION: AN ECOLOGICAL PERSPECTIVE

Ahmed Youssefagha, Chelsea Heaven,
Adrienne Luegers, Nancy Morales
and Wasantha Jayawardene
School of Public Health, Indiana University, US

ABSTRACT

The goal of this study is to examine the differences in diet and lifestyle risks between countries in the Middle East and North Africa (MENA) region identified as having a high, medium, and low prevalence of diabetes based on the regional average. During the past few decades, rapid economic development, urbanization, and social and lifestyle changes have contributed to increase of diabetes prevalence in the MENA region. On average, countries with high diabetes prevalence have higher per-capita income, lower population, and higher meat consumption than countries with medium and low prevalence. Countries with medium and low prevalence had significant increases in the consumption of kilocalories and fat from 1990-2007, while countries with high prevalence group did not have significant increases.

INTRODUCTION

The prevalence of Type II diabetes is expanding globally at an alarming rate. According to the World Health Organization (2009), more than 220 million people worldwide have been diagnosed with diabetes. Recently, it was estimated that globally by 2025, one person will die a diabetes-related death every ten seconds (International Diabetes Foundation (IDF), 2009). In addition to the devastating health consequences experienced by its victims, Type II diabetes is having a significant effect on economic systems worldwide. According to the IDF (2010), global healthcare expenditures related to diabetes treatment and prevention are expected to account for 11.6% of total healthcare costs in 2010. This is equivalent to spending roughly $376 billion worldwide for the costs related to diabetes in 2010 (IDF, 2010). It is estimated by the IDF that the costs of diabetes are equivalent to approximately $703 per person globally (2010). Although these costs encompass all forms of diabetes mellitus, Type II diabetes is responsible for at least 85-95% of all diabetes-related healthcare costs (IDF, 2010).

Currently, North America is experiencing the highest prevalence of Type II diabetes in the world, with a rate of 10.2% of the total population diagnosed (IDF, 2009). The Middle East is slightly behind North America, with a prevalence of Type II diabetes among 9.3% of the total population (IDF, 2009). It is projected by the IDF that mortality rates and disease burden globally will continue to increase unless immense changes are made throughout the world, particularly when it comes to eating habits and levels of physical activity. It is predicted that the world will see an average increase in death rate of 17% from diabetes-related health issues (IDF, 2010). There is grave concern for low and middle income countries in Africa and the Middle East, which may see diabetes-related death increases of 27% and 25%, respectively (IDF, 2010).

The region of focus in this ecological study is the Middle East. Currently, the Middle East region houses five of the top ten countries in the world with the highest prevalence of diabetes among adults aged 20 to 79 years (IDF, 2009). There is much speculation regarding the potential causative factors relating to the drastic increase in prevalence of diabetes among countries in the Middle East. A qualitative study by El-Kebbi & Engelgau (1994) deducted that during the past few decades, rapid economic development, urbanization, and social and lifestyle changes have contributed to the colossal increase of diabetes prevalence in the Middle East.

When considering rapid economic development, per capita income has increased dramatically in the last 20 years, particularly in the countries in which there is a higher prevalence of diabetes (Herman et al., 1997). Many studies have indicated that a higher socioeconomic status of a region will result in a greater incidence of diabetes rates. According to a study conducted by Mendez et al. (2005), urbanization and gross national income (GNI) were positively correlated in countries with a high prevalence of overweight women and negatively correlated with rates of underweight women among both urban and rural women in developing countries.

The shift of the Middle East region into increased urbanization is frequently emphasized when considering the high prevalence of diabetes. It is speculated that the increase in oil production in many countries in the Middle East over the past three decades has contributed to a shift in the way of life of many in the Middle East. This massive shift includes increased access to mass media, a decrease in physical activity as a result of new technologies related to transportation, work, and leisure; and increased access to a wide array of non-traditional foods throughout the year (Mendez & Popkin, 2004). This type of shift in the availability of resources, foods, and technology illustrates the concept of urbanization. According to Mendez & Popkin (2004), when urbanization occurs, several changes may take place. First, home food production and home food consumption decreases as less land is available for the growing of crops. The accessibility of less traditional foods increases with the proliferation of technological resources such as transportation and refrigeration. In addition to the previously mentioned elements of urbanization comes a heightening of mass media influence, which can influence the socio-culture, tastes, and preferences of a region (Chopra, Galbraith, & Darnton-Hill, 2002).

The concepts of rapid economic development and increased urbanization directly influence the social and lifestyle changes widely observed throughout the Middle East in the last three decades. Perhaps the most significant change in the lifestyles of Middle Eastern people is the shift in their food consumption patterns. It has often been reported that in the past, the traditional Middle Eastern diet consisted of high fiber foods that were low in fats, but is rapidly being replaced with highly processed, fat-laden foods that are high in carbohydrates, calories, and low in nutritional value. These types of foods are associated with a more Westernized diet and are reducing the consumption of fruits and vegetables (El-Kebbi & Engelgau, 1994). This modification of eating patterns is resulting in higher blood sugar levels, an increase in overweight and obese people, and ultimately, higher prevalence of diabetes in many countries in the Middle East region.

It was hypothesized by James Neel (1962) that people in the Middle East region might possess a "thrifty genotype" that causes a predisposition to diabetes. This "thrifty genotype" was utilized metabolically in the past for human survival in dry, harsh, desert-like climates in which the food supply was often scarce. Now in the Middle East, with the current overabundance of food, this "thrifty genotype" has ensued in a detrimental consequence to the health of people in the Middle East, resulting in a drastic increase of overweight, obesity, and the incidence of diabetes (Al-Lawati et al., 2002).

The goal of this study is to further examine the differences in diet and lifestyle between the specific countries in the Middle East with a high prevalence of diabetes as compared to the countries in the Middle East with a low prevalence of diabetes. The data sources in this study are based from findings by the IDF, WHO, and the Food and Agriculture Organization of the United Nations (FAO).

METHOD

Diabetes Prevalence Data

The prevalence percentage of diabetes in the Middle East and North Africa region (MENA) was calculated by staff of the International Diabetes Federation utilizing literature review data and in consultation with individual diabetes experts in each country (Sicree, Shaw, Zimmet, Bakder, Diabetes Institute, 2009). For the purposes of this study, we utilized the comparative prevalence rates instead of national prevalence rates. Comparative prevalence rates are calculated by comparing the diabetes rate of a specific country to the world population instead of the national population. The IDF recommends the use of the comparative prevalence when comparing diabetes rates between countries. The population data was collected from the United Nations Population Division, 2007. Table 1 provides the citations used for the diabetes prevalence data of MENA countries.

A full description of the finding and extrapolation process of diabetes prevalence data can be found in Appendix 1 of Sicree, Shaw, Zimmet, Bakder, & Diabetes Institute, 2009.

Selection of Prevalence Groups

The countries were grouped into a high, medium, and low diabetes prevalence based on the estimated comparative prevalence of diabetes in 2010. The mean estimated comparative diabetes prevalence for the MENA region is 10.5% with a standard deviation of 3.97 (IDF, 2009). Countries whose estimated diabetes prevalence was on or below the 25th percentile or lower was defined as "low," countries whose prevalence was in the between the 25th and 75th percentile was defined as "medium," and countries whose prevalence was on the 75th percentile or higher was defined as "high.

Table 1. Sources of Diabetes Prevalence Statistics

Country/Territory	Data Used	Screening Method	Diagnostic Criteria
Afghanistan	Pakistan	OGTT	WHO -1985
Algeria	Algeria (Malek et al., 2001)	OGTT	WHO -1985
Armenia	Turkey	2hBG	WHO -1999
Bahrain	Bahrain (Al-Mahroos et al., 1998)	OGTT	WHO -1985
Egypt	Egypt (Herman et al., 1995 and Arab, 1997)	OGTT/Post prandial GT	WHO -1985
Iran, Islamic Republic of	Iran (Azizi et al., 2003)	OGTT	WHO -1999
Iraq	Jordan	OGTT	WHO -1985
Jordan	Jordan (Ajlouni et al., 1998)	OGTT	WHO -1985
Kuwait	Kuwait (Abdella et al., 1998)	OGTT	WHO -1985
Lebanon	Lebanon (Salti et al., 1997)	OGTT	WHO -1985
Libya	Libya (Kadiki et al., 1999)	Registration	N/A
Morocco	Morocco (Tazi et al., 2003)	FBG/ SR	WHO -1980
Oman	Oman (Al-Lawati et al., 2002)	OGTT	WHO -1999
Pakistan	Pakistan (Shera et al., 1995, 1999a, 1999b)	OGTT	WHO -1985
Pakistan	Pakistan (Basit et al., 2002)	FBG	ADA -1997
Qatar	Bahrain	OGTT	WHO -1985
Saudi Arabiaa	Saudi Arabia (El Hazmi et al., 1998; Al-Nozha et al., 2004; Al-Nuaim, 1997)	OGTT	WHO -1985, ADA 1997,
Sudan	Sudan (Elbagir et al., 1996)	2hBG	WHO -1985
Syria	Syria (Albache, 2006)	OGTT	WHO -1999
Tunisia	Tunisia (Bougerra et al., 2007)	FBG	ADA -1997
United Arab Emirates	UAE (Malik et al., 2005)	OGTT	WHO -1999
United Arab Emirates	UAE (Saadi et al., 2007)	OGTT	WHO -1999
Yemen	Yemen (Al-Habori, 2004)	OGTT	WHO -1999

Countries in the low group were Afghanistan, Iran, Lebanon, Sudan, and Yemen. Countries in the medium prevalence group were Algeria, Armenia, Egypt, Iraq, Jordan, Libya, Morocco, Pakistan, Syria, and Tunisia. Countries in the high prevalence group were Bahrain, Oman, Qatar, Saudi Arabia, and United Arab Emirates.

Food Consumption Data

Datasets describing the average amount of calories, fat, and specific food groups available for consumption by an individual was obtained from the website of the FAO. The FAO assembled this data into a publication called the Food Balance Sheet (FAOSTAT, 2008). Data was collected by having officials from each country fill out questionnaires regarding the availability of food groups. The availability of calories and fat was extrapolated by detailing nutritional information about the availability of specific food groups. More detailed information about the methodology can be found from the latest Food Balance Sheet (FAOSTAT, 2008).

Therefore, these data describe how available each food group is to a population in grams/per person/per day. The actual consumption of the food groups may be lower due to food wastage, amount fed to pets, etc. The food groups include cereals (excluding beer), starchy roots, sugar & sweeteners, pulses, treenuts, oilcrops, vegetable oils, vegetables, fruit (excluding wine), stimulants, alcoholic beverages, meat, offal, animal fats, milk (excluding butter), eggs, and seafood.

Analysis of Food Consumption Data

The experimenters downloaded the full datasets from the FAO Statistics Division website (FAOSTAT, 2008). The experimenters copied the data from MENA countries into a separate excel sheet that had a similar layout to the original dataset. Both datasets describe the availability of food at 4 time periods.

The time periods are 1990-1992, 1995-1997, 2000-2002, 2005-2007. The experimenters made comparisons between diabetes prevalence groups by averaging the data at each time period based on diabetes prevalence groups. Data was missing from Bahrain, Oman, Qatar, Iraq, and Afghanistan.

Population and GDP Data

Data regarding population and GDP per capita were obtained from the World Bank. The World Bank 2010 World Development Indicators (2010) publication describes the GDP collection process as follows: "GDP per capita is gross domestic product divided by midyear population. GDP is the sum of gross value added by all resident producers in the economy plus any product taxes and minus any subsidies not included in the value of the products. It is calculated without making deductions for depreciation of fabricated assets or for depletion and degradation of natural resources. Data are in current U.S. dollars." (World Bank National Accounts Data, 2010)

The World Bank defines population statistics for a "total population" which "is based on the de facto definition of population, which counts all residents regardless of legal status or citizenship—except for refugees not permanently settled in the country of asylum, who are generally considered part of the population of their country of origin. The values shown are midyear estimates." (United Nations Population Division, 2009)

Analysis of GDP and Population Data

The extraction of GDP and Population data followed the same process described above for the Food Consumption Data. The experimenters utilized the GDP per capita and Population data from 1990-2009. For comparison purposes, the experimenters created a GDP index variable. This variable was created by standardizing GDP data points from 1990-2009 into z-scores and summing these z-scores to create an overall GDP index.

RESULTS

GDP and Population

The experimenters conducted two One-Way ANOVAs to compare the means of GDP per capita and Population between the High, Medium, and Low Diabetes Prevalence group. This analysis indicated that the High Diabetes Prevalence group had a higher GDP per capita than the Medium Prevalence and Low Prevalence group ($F(2, 57) = 741.51$, $p < 0.001$). There were no significant differences between the Medium and Low Prevalence Groups. Figure 1 illustrates the GDP per capita data from 1990-2009.

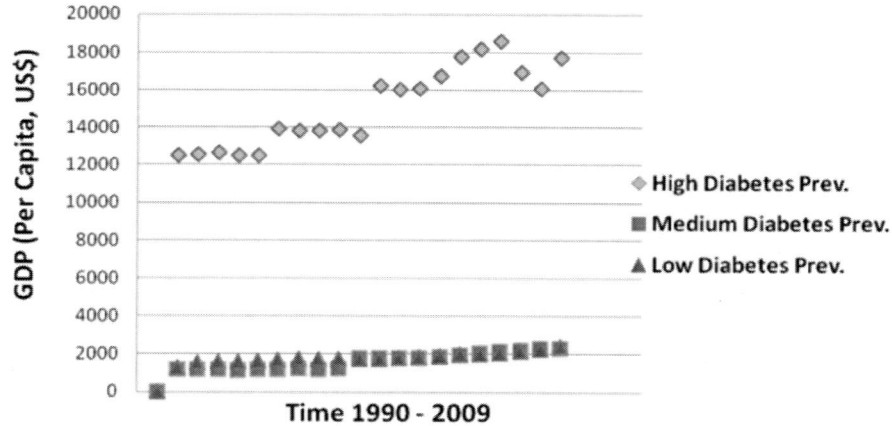

Figure 1. Gross Domestic Product per Capita, US$, 1990-2009.

Conversely, countries in the high diabetes group have lower population than the medium or low population groups ($F(2, 57) = 601.50$, $p < 0.001$). There were no significant differences between the medium and low prevalence groups. Figure 2 illustrates the Population data points from 1990-2009.

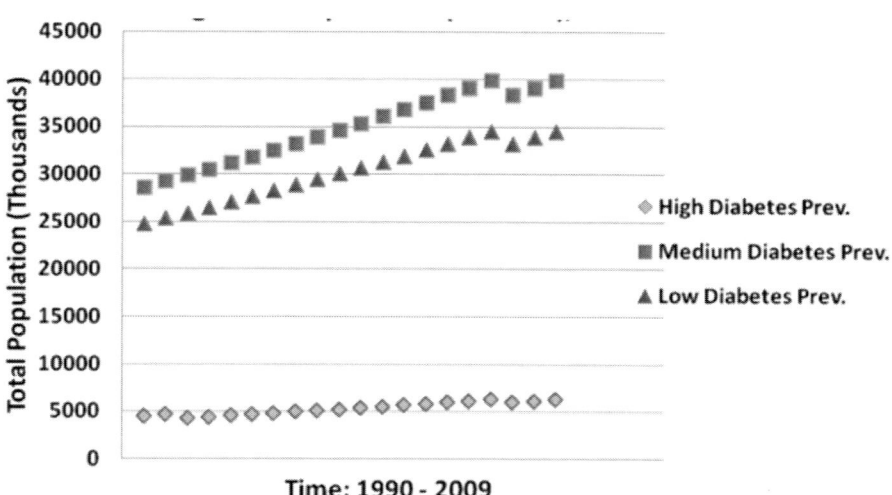

Figure 2. Population (in 000's), 1990-2009.

Consumption of Kilocalories and Fat

The experimenters performed paired-samples t-tests to evaluate if consumption of kilocalories and fat increased from 1990 to 2007 in diabetes prevalence countries. The medium diabetes prevalence group had a significant increases in kilocalorie and fat consumption from 1990-2007 ($t(8) = -4.08$, $p = .004$; $t(8) = -2.71$, $p = .026$). Countries in the low diabetes prevalence group had increased consumption of fat from 1990-2007 ($t(3) = -5.06$, $p = .0.015$). There were no differences in consumption from 1990-2007 in the high diabetes prevalence group.

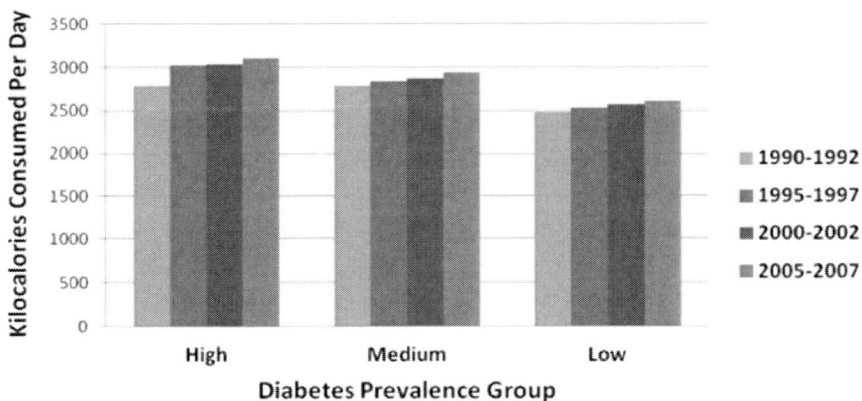

Figure 3. Consumption of Calories Per Day: 1990-2007.

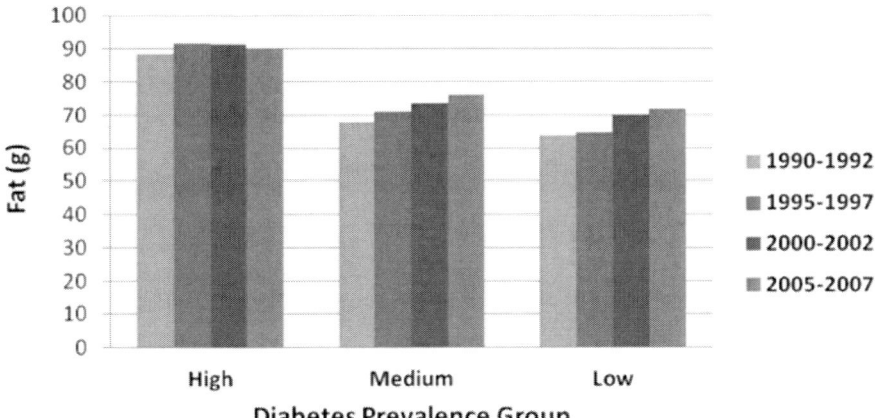

Figure 4. Consumption of Fat Per Day: 1990-2007.

The experimenters performed a One-Way ANOVA to see if diabetes prevalence groups differed in their average consumption of kilocalories and fat. There were no significant differences found between the three prevalence groups consumption of fat and calories. ($F(2, 13) = 1.076$, $p = n.s$; $F(2, 14) = 1.58$, $p = n.s.$). Figure 3 depicts the amount of kilocalories available to each prevalence group at four time periods (1990-1992, 1995-1997, 2000-2002, 2005-2007). Figure 4 depicts the availability of fat available for each person per day at the four time periods.

Consumption of Food Groups

The experimenters performed a One-Way ANOVA to see if there were any differences between the types of food available between diabetes prevalence groups. We found that in 2005-2007, governments in the high diabetes prevalence countries made more meat available to their population than the medium and low prevalence groups ($F(2, 12) = 11.85$, $p = 0.001$). There were no significant differences with any other food groups. Figure 5 depicts the availability of food groups between the diabetes prevalence groups in 2005-2007.

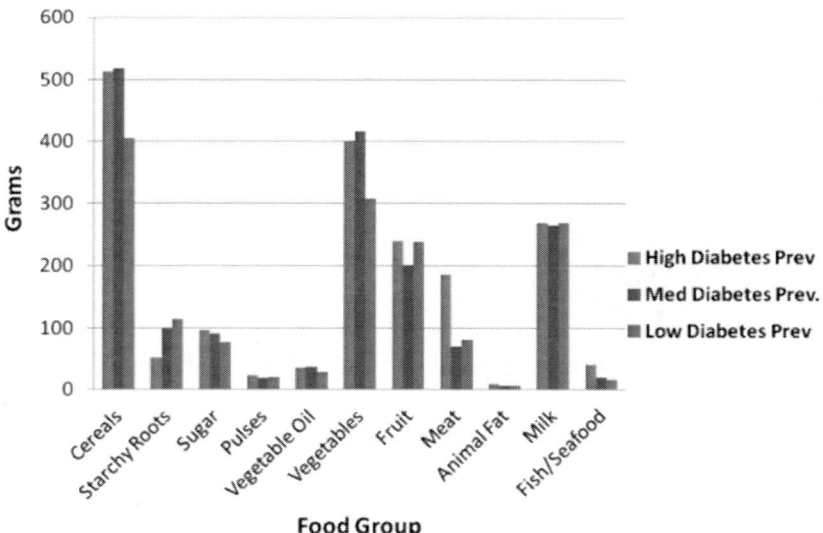

Figure 5. Food Groups Available Per Person per day, 2005-2007.

GDP and Food Consumption

To investigate the relationship between GDP and food consumption, the experimenters ran Pearson's correlations on the GDP index variable with food consumption variables. Overall in the MENA region, in the 2005-2007 timeframe higher GDP is related to greater availability of pulses, meat, and fish/seafood ($r = .55, p = .031$; $r = .90, p < 0.001$; $r = .74, p < 0.001$, respectively).

In the high diabetes prevalence group, higher GDP is related to higher availability of pulses, meat, and fish/seafood ($r = .99, p = .040$; $r = .90, p < 0.001$; $r = .99, p = 0.048$). In the medium diabetes prevalence, GDP was not related to the availability of any food group. In the low diabetes prevalence group, higher GDP is related to higher availability of starchy roots, sugar, vegetable oil, and meat ($r = .97, p = .028$; $r = .99, p < 0.008$; $r = .97, p = 0.025$; $r = .98, p = .016$, respectively).

DISCUSSION

The finding that countries in the high diabetes prevalence group have lower populations and higher GDP suggests these countries have a high proportion of their population at risk for diabetes. This finding suggests that there may be some systemic issues in distribution of wealth and food that could be looked at in future research.

The finding that countries in the medium diabetes prevalence group had a significant increase in consumption of kcals and fat from 1990-2007 and countries in the high group did not suggest that countries in the medium prevalence group may be on their way to developing a high prevalence rate in the future. Similarly, countries in the low diabetes prevalence group had a significant increase in fat consumption from 1990-2007.

Countries in the high diabetes group have more meat available. Overall in the region, higher GDP is related to increased availability of pulses (beans), meat, and fish/seafood. In the high group, higher GDP is related to higher availability of pulses, meat, and fish/seafood, in the medium group, higher GDP is not related to increased availability of food. In the low group, higher GDP is related to more availability of starchy roots, pulses, vegetable oil, and meat. This data could indicate that countries with a higher GDP may have greater levels of disposable income in which to purchase foods considered richer or more calorie latent. These types of foods may be thought of as more of a luxury and may represent a certain superior social status. It is recommended that future research should investigate the symbolism of foods thought of as more of a luxury relating to class status within the culture of the Middle East as a means of understanding decisions behind health behavior.

The results of the current study should be interpreted with caution because of the problem of ecological fallacy. In this study, the ecological fallacy would provide the assumption that aggregate data (i.e., population data, food statistics, etc.) applies to all individuals living in the country (Greenland & Robins, 1994). Therefore, this data should be interpreted primarily for future hypothesis testing.

The inconsistent quality of the data is another limitation to the quality of these findings. Several countries intended for inclusion in the analysis were lacking in food security data, as well as consistent time parameters for data analysis. The data analyzed is based on the averages of the experimenter defined experiment groups. Based on this information, the findings from this study should be considered with further caution.

Another significant limitation is the fact that the high, medium, and low prevalence diabetes groups were selected by the experimenter. Future research should use more sophisticated methods to select prevalence groups in order to gain accurate information on the differences between countries with high and low diabetes prevalence.

Despite these limitations, the current study suggests that there may be a relationship between types of food consumed and prevalence of diabetes in the MENA region, and that this relationship may be related to systemic government issues of food availability. Future research should investigate these findings with detailed data collection and analysis in order to formulate strategies to prevent the fast growing rates of diabetes in the MENA region.

Conclusion

This ecological analysis suggests that there may be a relationship between types of food consumed and prevalence of diabetes in the MENA region, and that this relationship may be related to systemic government issues of food availability and economic development. The finding that countries in the high prevalence group have lower populations and higher GDP per capita suggests that there may be some systemic issues in the distribution of wealth and food that result in some countries having increased access to a food supply that promotes diabetes. The finding that countries in the medium and low diabetes prevalence groups had significant increases in consumption of kcals and fat in the past 20 years suggests that these countries may develop a high diabetes prevalence rate in the future. Future research should investigate these findings with sound data collection methods and analysis in order to formulate strategies to prevent the growing rates of diabetes in the MENA regions.

REFERENCES

Abdella, N., Al Arouj, M., Al Nakhi, A., Al Assoussi, A., & Moussa, M. (1998). Non-insulindependent diabetes in Kuwait: Prevalence rates and associated risk factors. *Diabetes Res Clin Pract*, *42*(3), 187-196.

Albache N. *personal communication.*

Al-Habori, M., Al-Mamari, M., & Al-Meeri, A. (2004). Type II Diabetes Mellitus and impaired glucose tolerance in Yemen: Prevalence, associated metabolic changes, and risk factors. *Diabetes Res Clin Pract*, *65*(3), 275-281.

Al-Lawati, J.A., Al Riyami, A.M., Mohammed, A.J., & Jousilahti, P. (2002). Increasing prevalence of diabetes mellitus in Oman. *Diabet Med*, *19*(11), 954-957.

Al-Lawati, J. A., Al Riyami, A. M., Mohammed, A. J., & Jousilahti, P. (2002). Increasing prevalence of diabetes mellitus in Oman. *Diabetic Medicine*, *19*(11), 954-957.

Al-Mahroos, F. & McKeigue, P.M. (1998). High prevalence of diabetes in Bahrainis. Associations with ethnicity and raised plasma cholesterol. *Diabetes Care*, *21*(6), 936-942.

Al-Nozha, M.M., Al-Maatouq, M.A., Al-Mazrou, Y.Y., Al-Harthi, S.S., Arafah, M.R., Khalil, M.Z. et al. (2004). Diabetes mellitus in Saudi Arabia.. *Saudi Med J.*, 25(11), 1603-10.

Al-Nuaim, A.R. (1997). Prevalence of glucose intolerance in urban and rural communities in Saudi Arabia. *Diabet Med.*, 14(7), 595-602.

Azizi, F., Salehi, P., Etemadi, A., & Zahedi-Asl, S. (2003). Prevalence of metabolic syndrome in an urban population: Tehran lipid and glucose study. *Diabetes Res Clin Pract*, *61*(1), 29-37.

Basit, A., Hydrie, M.Z., Ahmed, K., & Hakeem, R. (2002). Prevalence of diabetes, impaired fasting glucose, and associated risk factors in a rural area of Baluchistan province according to new ADA criteria. *J Pak Med Assoc*, *52*(8), 357-360.

Bouguerra, R., Alberti, H., Salem, L.B., Rayana, C.B., Atti, J.E., & Gaigi, S. (2007). The global diabetes pandemic: The Tunisian experience. *Eur J Clin Nutr, 61*(2), 160-165.

Elbagir, M., Eltom, M., Elmahadi, E., Kadam, I., & Berne, C. (1996). A population-based study of the prevalence of diabetes and impaired glucose tolerance in adults in Northern Sudan. *Diabetes Care, 19*(10), 1126-1128.

El-Hazmi, M., Warsy, A., Al-Swailem, A., Al-Swailem, A., & Sulaimani, R. (1998). Diabetes mellitus as a health problem in Saudi Arabia. *Eastern Mediterranean Health Journal, 4*(1), 58-67.

El-Kebbi, I. M. & Engelgau, M. M. (1994). The Burden of Diabetes and its Complications in the Middle East and Eastern Mediterranean Region - *The Epidemiology of Diabetes Mellitus*

Imad M. El-Kebbi, I. M., & Engelgau, M. M. (2006). The Burden of Diabetes and its Complications in the Middle East and Eastern Mediterranean Region. In Jean-Marie Ekoé, J., Rewers, M., Williams, R., & Zimmet P. *The Epidemiology of Diabetes Mellitus* (2nd Ed., pp. 121-131). Online: John Wiley & Sons, Ltd.

ESS: Food Balance Sheets [online]. (2010) [cited 2010 November 19, 2010]. Available from: *http://www.fao.org/economic/ess/publications-studies/publications/food-balance-sheets/en/et al.*

Food and Agriculture Organization of the United Nations. FAOSTAT [online]. (2008) [cited 2010 November 5). Available from: *http://faostat.fao.org/site/291/default.aspx.* (Good and Agriculture Organization of the United Nations (FAO). (2007, May). Workshop on Supply Utilization Accounts and Food Balance Sheets. Dushanbe, Tajikistan.

Greenland, S. & Robins, J. (1994). Invited commentary: Ecologic studies—Biases, misconceptions, and counterexamples. *American Journal of Epidemiology, 139*(8), 747-760.

Herman, W., Ali, M., Aubert, R., Engelgau, M., Kenny, S., & Gunter, E. (1995). Diabetes mellitus in Egypt: Risk factors and prevalence. *Diabetic Medicine, 12,* 1126-1131.

International Diabetes Federation. (2000). *IDF Diabetes Atlas, 1st ed.* Accessed on 07/05/2013

International Diabetes Federation. (2003). *IDF Diabetes Atlas, 2nd ed.* Accessed on 07/05/2013

International Diabetes Federation. (2007). *IDF Diabetes Atlas, 3rd ed.* Accessed on 07/06/2013

International Diabetes Federation. (2009). *IDF Diabetes Atlas: 4th ed.* Accessed on 07/06/2013

Kadiki, O.A. & Roaed, R.B. (1999). Epidemiological and clinical patterns of diabetes mellitus in Benghazi, Libyan Arab Jamahiriya. *East Mediterr Health J*, *5*(1), 6-13.

Malek, R., Belateche, F., Laouamri, S., Hamdi-Cherif, M., Touabti, A., & Bendib, W. (2001). Prevalence of Type II diabetes mellitus and glucose intolerance in the Setif area (Algeria). *Diabetes Metab*, *27*(2 Pt. 1), 164-171.

Malik, M., Bakir, A., Saab, B.A., Roglic, G., & King, H. (2005). Glucose intolerance and associated factors in the multi-ethnic population of the United Arab Emirates: Results of a national survey. *Diabetes Res Clin Pract*, *69*(2), 188-195.

Mendez, M.A., Monteiro, C.A., & Popkin, B.M. (2005). Overweight exceeds underweight among women in most developing countries. *The American Journal of Clinical Nutrition*, *81*(3), 714 -721.

Mendez, M., Popkin, A., & Barry, M. (2004). Globalization, urbanization, and nutritional changes in the developing world. *eJADE: Electronic Journal of Agricultural and Development Economics* [Online serial], *1*(2), 220-241.

Chopra, M., Galbraith, S., & Darnton-Hill, I. (2002). A global response to a global problem: The epidemic of overnutrition. *Bulletin of the World Health Organization*, *80*, 952–958.

Neel, J.V. (1962). Diabetes mellitus: A "thrifty " genotype rendered detrimental by "progress "? *American Journal of Human Genetics*, *14*, 353-362.

Saadi, H., Carruthers, S.G., Nagelkerke, N., Al-Maskari, F., Afandi, B., & Reed, R. (2007). Prevalence of diabetes mellitus and its complications in a population-based sample in Al Ain, United Arab Emirates. *Diabetes Res Clin Pract*, *78*(3), 369-377.

Salti, S., Khogali, M., Alam, S., Abu Haidar, N., & Masri, A. (1997). Epidemiology of diabetes mellitus in relation to other cardiovascular risk factors in Lebanon. *Eastern Mediterranean Health Journal*, *3*, 462-471.

Satman, I., Yilmaz, T., Sengul, A., Salman, S., Salman, F., & Uygur, S. (1997). Population based study of diabetes and risk characteristics in Turkey: Results of the Turkish diabetes epidemiology study (TURDEP). *Diabetes Care* 2002; 25(9):1551-6.

Shera, A.S., Rafique, G., Khawaja, I.A., Baqai, S., & King, H. (1999). Pakistan national diabetes survey: Prevalence of glucose intolerance and associated factors in Baluchistan province. *Diabetes Res Clin Pract*, *44*(1), 49-58.

Shera, A.S., Rafique, G., Khwaja, I.A., Ara, J., Baqai, S., & King, H. (1995). Pakistan national diabetes survey: Prevalence of glucose intolerance and associated factors in Shikarpur, Sindh Province. *Diabet Med*, *12*(12), 1116-1121.

Shera, A.S., Rafique, G., Khwaja, I.A., Baqai, S., Khan, I.A., & King, H. (1999). Pakistan national diabetes survey: Prevalence of glucose intolerance and associated factors in North West Frontier Province (NWFP) of Pakistan. *J Pak Med Assoc*, *49*(9), 206-211.

Sicree, R., Shaw, J., Zimmet, P., & Baker IDI Heart and Diabetes Institute. (2009). The Global Burden: Diabetes and Impaired Glucose Tolerance. In *IDF Diabetes Atlas* (4th Ed., pp. 1-105). Brussels, Belgium: International Diabetes Federation

Tazi, M.A., Abir-Khalil, S., Chaouki, N., Cherqaoui, S., Lahmouz, F., & Srairi, J.E. (2000). Prevalence of the main cardiovascular risk factors in Morocco: results of a National Survey. *J Hypertens*, *21*(5), 897-903.

The Global Burden Diabetes Atlas. (2010). *IDF Diabetes Atlas* [online]. (2010) [cited 2010 November 10]. Available from: *http://www. diabetesatlas.org/content/global-burden*.

United Nations Population Division. (2009). United Nations Population Division. 2009. *World Population Prospects: The 2008 Revision*. New York, United Nations, Department of Economic and Social Affairs.

United Nations, Population Division. (2007). *World Population Prospects: The 2006 Revision*. Geneva, Switzerland.

William, H.H., Aubert, R.E., Ali, M.A., Sous, E.S., & Badran, A. (1997). Diabetes mellitus in Egypt: Risk factors, prevalence, and future burden. *Eastern Mediterranean Health Journal*, *3*(1), 144-148.

World Bank (2010). Data Catalog: National Accounts Data. Available at http://datacatalog.worldbank.org/ Accessed on 07/21/2011.

World Bank Publications. World Development Indicators [online]. (2010) [cited 2010 November 19]. Available from *http://publications. worldbank. org/index.php?main_page=product_info&cPath=0&products_id=23799*.

In: Contemporary Issues in Public Health　　ISBN: 978-1-63117-933-4
Editors: S.G. Obeng, A. Youssefagha et al.　© 2014 Nova Science Publishers, Inc.

Chapter 3

HEPATITIS B AND C IN REFUGEES FROM NORTHEAST AFRICA: THE NEED FOR SCREENING

Ahmed Youssefagha, Wasantha Jayawardene and David Lohrmann
Indiana University, US

ABSTRACT

The WHO estimates that 2 billion people have been infected with hepatitis-B and about 180 million people infected with hepatitis-C worldwide. Middle-East and North-Africa have a high prevalence of hepatitis B and C, while these regions also serve as one of the major origins for refugees. Although overall incidence of hepatitis B in the U.S. is decreasing and incidence of hepatitis C is almost leveled off during past decade, the trend may not be the same in relation to refugees. Screenings of these diseases are not performed before departure or after arrival. The implications of this review indicate a need for screening of hepatitis, immunization against Hepatitis-B, and comprehensive treatment and follow-up of care for refugees positive with the infection.

BACKGROUND

Viral hepatitis, specifically hepatitis B and C virus, is a major health issue facing the world today (World Health Organization, 2005; Sy & Jamal, 2006; Chironna et al., 2003). It is a viral pandemic (Lauer & Walker, 2001). Hepatitis C virus (HCV) and hepatitis B virus (HBV) infections are commonly found worldwide. Approximately 3% of the world's population has HCV (WHO, 1999). The World Health Organization estimates that 2 billion people have been infected with hepatitis-B and about 180 million people infected with hepatitis-C worldwide. More than 350 million have chronic hepatitis-B and 130 million have chronic hepatitis-C infection. Early exposure to HBV creates the highest risk for chronic infection, but HCV is also associated with chronic infections (WHO, 2005). Chronic carriers are susceptible to cirrhosis of the liver and possibly the development of hepatocellular carcinoma (HCC). Because of the asymptomatic nature of the disease, there is long incubation period between infection and evidence of infection, such as liver failure (Centers for Disease Control and Prevention, 1998). Chronic HCV infection has become a main implication for liver transplantation in the developed world (Lauer & Walker, 2001, Kew et al., 2004). Egypt has the highest prevalence of HCV in the world, and HCV is the leading cause of liver cancer in Egypt and the U.S. (Poustchi et al., 2010). A study showed that 20% of those over 30 years of age in the Nile delta region of Egypt tested positive for the HCV antibodies (Nafeh et al., 2000). With Egypt as a major hub from which refugees travel (United Nations Commissioner for Refugees, 2010), it is important that the health issue of HCV is properly addressed.

Transmission of Viral Hepatitis

The World Health Organization states that HCV in developed countries is mostly transmitted through blood transfusions, blood products, or organs, sharing needles with someone who is infected, haemodialysis, risky sexual behaviors, and having medical or dental procedures with improperly sterilized equipment (WHO, 1999). In developing countries, however, the mode of transmission includes similar methods which include receiving blood, blood products, or organs which have not been screened as well as undergoing medical and dental procedures with unsterilized equipment, but also inadequately sterilized needles and the use of unsterilized instruments for ritual procedures such as scarification, tattooing, circumcision, etc. (WHO,

1999, Bojuwoye, 1997, McCarthy et al., 1994). Marginal risk has been shown between mother and child and in between household members (Chironna et al., 2003).

McCarthy et al. (1994) ran a serosurvey to determine the prevalence of HBV and HCV in southern Sudan. He found that of his sample of around 650 subjects, 26% were positive for anti-HBsAg. He also found that those who were positive were older and had a history of scarification than those who were negative. Only around 3% of the sample showed a positive on the anti-HCV immunoblot test. There was not a correlation between older subjects and HCV as there was with HBV. The high prevalence of HBV in this area is probably due to the tribal practices of tattooing and scarification, probably transmitted before the start of sexual activity. The low prevalence of HCV may account for the young age of the sample, just at a mean of 16 plus or minus 10 years.

In parts of Africa, circumcision is becoming more popular based on the presumption that it will reduce the risk of transmission of human immunodeficiency virus (HIV) (Auvert et al., 2005). A study by Bongaarts et al. (1989) found that African countries with higher circumcision rates had lower overall rates of HIV. However, male circumcision has been listed as a potential source of hepatitis infections (WHO, 1999, Bojuwoye, 1997, McCarthy et al., 1994). Within our area of interest of northeast Africa, Bongaarts et al. (1989) shows higher rates of male circumcision and lower rates of HIV, but some of the highest rates of hepatitis have been reported there (WHO, 1999).

A refugee is a person who "owing to a well-founded fear of being persecuted for reasons of race, religion, nationality, membership of a particular social group, or political opinion, is outside the country of his nationality, and is unable to or, owing to such fear, is unwilling to avail himself of the protection of that country" (The 1951 Refugee Convention, UNHCR; Figure-1).

The status of political asylum is granted by the U.S. Citizenship and Immigration Services to an alien residing in the United States as a result of a well-founded fear of persecution in the individual's country because of race, religion, ethnic group, or social group. This status is similar to refugee status. The difference is that refugees are granted their status abroad while individuals seeking asylum apply after they enter the United States. Generally speaking, an immigrant is considered to be a person who chooses to leave his or her country and is usually seeking employment and education opportunities that are either not present or are inadequate within their own country.

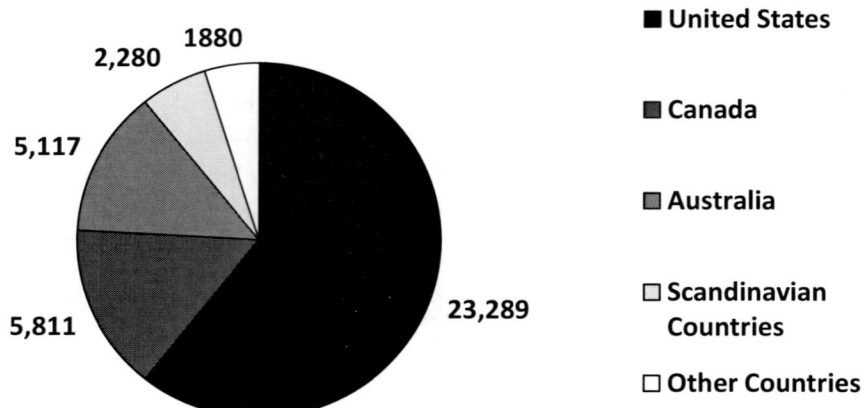

Source: United States Department of State, United States Department of Homeland Security, United States Department of Health and Human Services (2006). Proposed refugee admissions for fiscal year 2007 - Report to the congress: Submitted on behalf of the president of the United States to the committees on the judiciary United States senate and United States house of representatives in fulfillment of the requirements of section 207(e)(1)-(7) of the Immigration and Nationality Act.

Figure 1. UNIHCR Resettlement Statistics by Resettlement County during Year 2005.

The rates of HCV and HBV among refugees are relatively high in comparison with general population, but since the number of refugees in a total population is minute, they could be potentially overlooked.

We can examine the raw data of refugee arrivals by country of nationality to examine the pattern of arrivals. The data is available from the Department of Homeland Security through the Office of Immigration Statistics. The rates of refugee arrival have fluctuated greatly in the last ten years. In 2001, the rates dramatically decline and only in the past few years have they started to increase again. Within our area of focus, the majority of refugees that came to the U.S. last year are from Somalia. Eritrea had the next largest group of refugees, followed by Sudan and Ethiopia with less than 1000 from each country, and lastly, less that 100 from each country came from Djibouti and Kenya. Looking at the same raw data, we can also see that over the course of this last decade, the majority of refugees are from Somalia. In alignment with the data from the previous year, refugees from Ethiopia and Sudan are the next largest groups to resettle in the U.S. this decade (DHS, 2010).

Hepatitis B and C in the U.S.

The population most commonly seen at risk for HCV in the U.S. is injection drug users (IDUs) (CDC, 1998). IDUs frequently share needles and because of the asymptomatic nature of the HCV, can often go long periods of time without feelings of sickness and, therefore, can pass the infection on to others. Just as we need to screen refugees before coming to U.S. or on arrival, IDUs need to be screened as well. Drug treatment facilities that have the most contact with this particular population should focus some effort on reducing the risk of transmission between IDUs by screening and offering or referring treatment for HCV as well as treatment for addiction (Vassilev et al., 2004). Udeagu Pratt et al. (2002) found that only around half of the drug treatment centers in New York City had HCV screening in their programs. Nationwide, some 40% of the drug treatment centers in a sample were unable to estimate the number of clients who had been screened for HCV (Vassilev et al., 2004). In surveillance reports from the CDC, it is documented that hepatitis B overall incidence is declining in the U.S., although HCV rates have leveled off since 2003 (Figures 2 and 3).

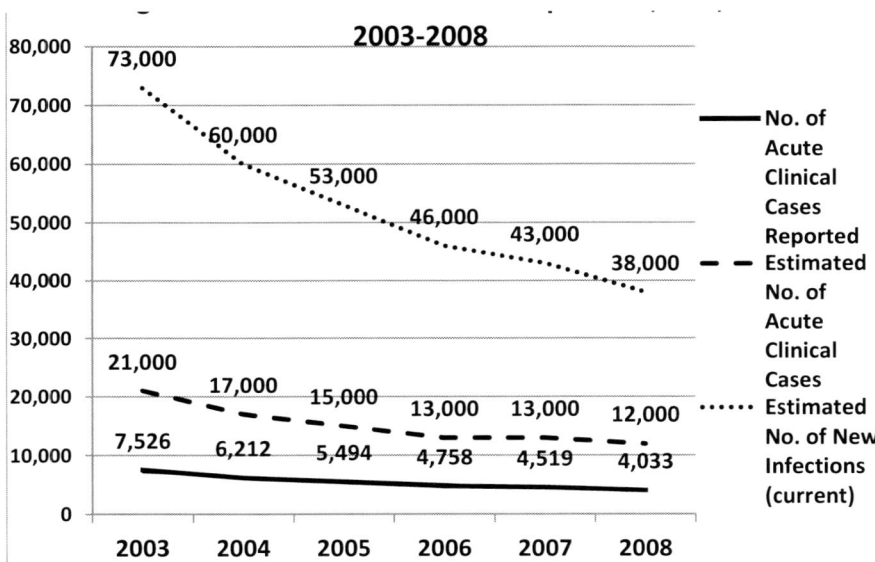

Source: Centers for Disease Control and Prevention. (2010). Viral Hepatitis Statistics & Surveillance: Disease Burden from Viral Hepatitis A, B, and C in the United States. Retrieved from http://www.cdc.gov/hepatitis/Statistics/index.htm

Figure 2. Disease Burden from Hepatitis B, S., 2003-2008.

In the U.S., chronic liver disease and cirrhosis is the 12th leading cause of death (Xu et al., 2010). Our previous research states that HBV and HCV are the leading causes of chronic liver disease and cirrhosis, and a major implication for liver transplantation (WHO, 2005, CDC, 1998, Lauer & Walker, 2001, Kew et al., 2004). It should be noted that there is a contrast in the fairly low rates of infection in the U.S. and seemingly high rates of death from chronic liver disease and cirrhosis, since it is the 12th leading cause (Table 1).

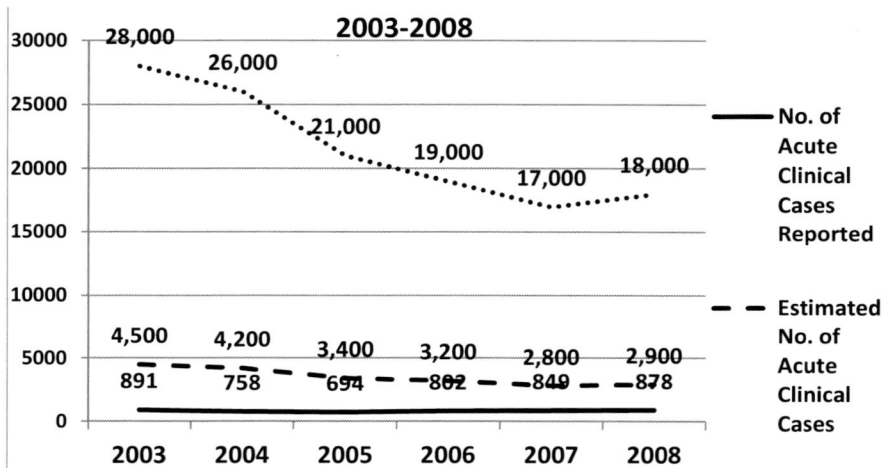

Source: Centers for Disease Control and Prevention. (2010). Viral Hepatitis Statistics & Surveillance: Disease Burden from Viral Hepatitis A, B, and C in the United States. Retrieved from http://www.cdc.gov/hepatitis/Statistics/index.htm

Figure 3. Disease Burden from Hepatitis C, U.S., 2003-2008.

Table 1. Disease Burden from Hepatitis B and C, U.S.: Research Findings, 1999-2008

Disease Burden	Hepatitis B	Hepatitis C
Percent Ever Infected (1)	4.3% - 5.6%	1.3% - 1.9%
Number of Persons Living with Chronic Infection in Millions (2)	0.8 - 1.4	2.7–3.9
Annual Number of Chronic Liver Disease Deaths associated with Viral Hepatitis (3)	3,000	12,000

Sources: (1) McQuillan et al. (1999) and Armstrong et al. (2006).
(2) CDC (2008) and Armstrong et al. (2006).
(3) Vogt et al. (2007); Manos et al. (2008) and Wise et al. (2008).

Hepatitis B and C Virus in Refugees

Studies in the U.S., Italy, Greece, France, and Australia all show that the rates of these viral infections are high in their populations of refugees. Several studies of Sudanese refugees in the U.S. after migration yielded similar results. Museru & Franco-Paredes (2009) found that 23% of mostly Sudanese refugees that came to a travel clinic in Atlanta tested positive for HBsAg, the surface antigen that is present when exposure to HBV has occurred. Museru et al. (2010) revisited this area of interest using retrospective descriptive study methods. Museru et al. (2010) looked at the population of refugees that came to resettle in the state of Georgia between 2003 and 2007 and found that 10.7% of those screened tested positive for HBsAg. The majority (71%) of the refugees included originated from Africa. It should be pointed out that in the particular county of DeKalb in which the refugees that were screened reside, of the 1,569 total cases of hepatitis exposure, 680 of those cases are of refugees. This results in an overwhelming 43.3% of the cases of hepatitis B in that county from refugees alone.

A study out of Minnesota by Lifson et al. (2002) discovered similar results; a high prevalence of the HBsAg, but at lower rates than the Atlanta travel clinic, at only 8% of the sub-Saharan refugee population. Although the sub-Saharan refugees in this study did not include any from Sudan, it is still important to point out the high prevalence of exposure to hepatitis B in a similar area of Africa. The prevalence of HBsAg among refugees in Italy, mostly from Africa, is similar as well. Tafuri et al. (2010) screened 529 refugees for HBsAg, anti-HBc, anti-HCV, and anti-HIV virus antibodies that were staying at asylum centers. He found 8.3% to be HBsAg positive, with 45.6% having anti-HBc antibodies, which may indicate past infection. Around 4.5% were positive for anti-HCV, indicating an exposure hepatitis C.

A second study out of Italy sampled Kurdish refugees from Iraq and Turkey (Chironna et al., 2003). A sample consisting of 1005, mostly male, refugees housed in a camp in Puglia were screened to assess the prevalence of viral hepatitis (A, E, B, and C). The majority (nearly 94%) was positive for the antigen associated with hepatitis A, indicating past infection, but no current symptoms of infection at arrival. Hepatitis E antigens were found in around 15% of the refugee population, higher in those from Iraq, and no antigens were found in either Iraqi or Turkish refugees under the age of ten. Anti-HBsAg markers were in around 4% of the sample, but higher at almost 7% of the Turkish refugees, and highest in the above 30 years of age group. Only 14 of the sample had been vaccinated against HBV, equating to around 10% of the under ten years old population. Since there are lower rates of HBV among children, it seems that vertical transmission is not a main factor in infection for this sample.

Refugees in Athens, Greece were screened for hepatitis B and C as a public health measure. Roussos et al. (2003) found that of the 130 refugees in the study, 15.4% were positive for HBsAg, and 53.1% were positive for anti-HBc, indicating previous exposure, but not necessarily a current infection. Three individuals in the populations were positive for anti-HCV (the antigen associated with infection of HCV) or 2.3%. Most of the refugees in the sample were from Albania or Eastern Europe; eight of the subjects were from Africa. Of the eight, two were positive for anti-HBc (25%) and one was positive for anti-HCV (12.5%).

Hepatitis Screening and Immunizations Among Refugees

A disproportionate number of diseases effect refugees in the United States (Barnett, 2004). Refugees come to the U.S. from countries with relatively high rates of hepatitis infections where rates vary widely based on country of origin (Chironna et al., 2003; see Table 2). In poorer countries, the vaccination of HBV in children is limited due to the lack of government funds (Benson & Donahue, 2007). Screening for HCV is not performed before departure or after arrival. Hepatitis B virus (HBV) is screened for after arrival, but only when indicated (Barnett, 2004). Form DS-2053 is the pre-departure screening for immigrants and refugees to enter the U.S (Figure 4). It includes screening for Class A and Class B conditions. Class A conditions include infectious tuberculosis, human, immunodeficiency virus, syphilis, gonorrhea, physical and mental disorders, etc. Class B conditions include Class A conditions that have been treated (United State Department of State, 1991). No screening for HBV or HCV is required.

Once a refugee has arrived to the U.S., it is voluntary to complete a domestic screening (Cochran et al., 2007; see Figure 4). Blanchet et al., (2003) states the importance of screening due to the chronic nature of the disease and its potential to cause morbidity. Screening is also promoted by the WHO; however, no strategies are currently in place to prevent or control viral hepatitis (WHO, 2005). In addition, the reliability of the screening procedures and the effectiveness of treatment when given early in the infection are also rationale for widespread screening (Blanchet et al., 2003).

The use of immunizations to combat the incidence of HBV is primary in preventing the spread of the infection. The WHO estimates the utilization of immunization of most countries in the world. The record we examined estimated immunization coverage for hepatitis B of one year olds in countries around the world (WHO, n.d.). Most of the countries of our interest (Somalia, Sudan, Ethiopia, Kenya, Eritrea, and Djibouti) are shown to be offered to their citizens, but only in the last decade. There is no data available for Somalia. Eritrea has the highest estimated coverage at 99% in the last year and nearly 90% each year since reporting started in 2002, followed by Djibouti at 89% last year with at a rate of 88% in the previous year and only 25% in the first year of reported immunizations in 2007. Sudan, Kenya, and Ethiopia have lower rates between 75% and 80% estimations of coverage this past year. Interestingly, Ethiopia, Djibouti, and Sudan are shown to only to be immunizing in the past four years or less, with Sudan and Eritrea reports only dating back to 2002. This is of concern because it could be concluded that the most children greater than 10 years of age only have not been vaccinated against hepatitis B, therefore having risk of infection and, therefore, risk of chronic liver disease and cirrhosis.

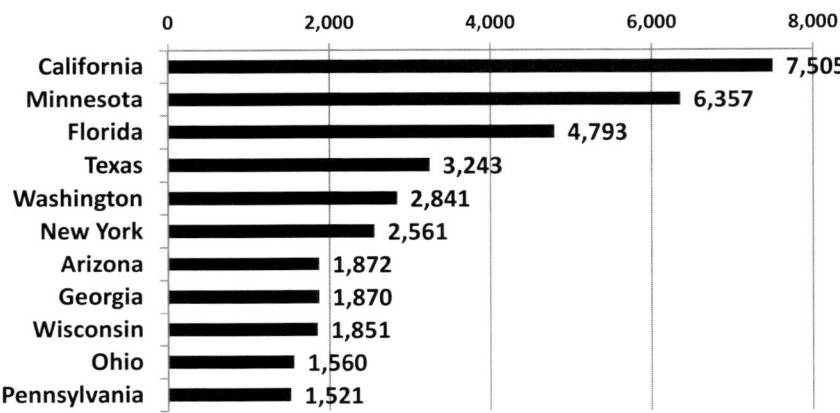

Source: United States Department of State, United States Department of Homeland Security, United States Department of Health and Human Services (2006). Proposed refugee admissions for fiscal year 2007 - Report to the congress: Submitted on behalf of the president of the United States to the committees on the judiciary United States senate and United States house of representatives in fulfillment of the requirements of section 207(e)(1)-(7) of the Immigration and Nationality Act.

Figure 4. Refugee Arrivals by State of Initial Resettlement in the U.S., 2005.

Screening and immunization are highly important in decreasing the incidence of viral hepatitis, in particular HBV for which there is a vaccination for, and for HCV to reduce the risk of transmission (Chironna et al., 2003). In the study in southern Sudan by McCarty et al. (1994), immunization of HBV could help prevent the transmission and rapid spread of the virus during tribal practices if immunization was done at birth.

Table 2. Country of Origin and Refugee Arrivals by Median Age and Gender, U.S., 2005

Rank Number of Arrivals	Country of Origin	Refugees Admitted	Median Age	% Females	% Males
1	Former Soviet Union	11,175	28.4	50.40%	49.60%
2	Somalia	10,405	21.1	48.40%	51.60%
3	Laos	8,517	20.1	50.50%	49.50%
4	Cuba	6,356	33	47.30%	52.70%
5	Liberia	4,289	21	55.10%	44.90%
6	Sudan	2,205	22.3	40.80%	59.20%
7	Vietnam	2,084	25.4	46.10%	53.90%
8	Iran	1,849	32.3	47.10%	52.90%
9	Ethiopia	1,665	25.2	47.60%	52.40%
10	Burma	1,447	24.7	45.10%	54.90%
11	Afghanistan	902	23.8	47.70%	52.30%
13	Sierra Leone	829	28.2	52.20%	47.80%
14	Democratic Republic of Congo	424	19.4	46.50%	53.50%
15	Eritrea	329	27.4	24.30%	75.70%
16	Colombia	323	25.1	51.40%	48.60%
17	Burundi	214	18.4	45.80%	54.20%
18	Iraq	198	27.8	39.90%	60.10%
19	Rwanda	183	22.6	50.80%	49.20%
20	Former Yugoslavia	138	30.9	52.20%	47.80%
21	Togo	72	23.6	50.00%	50.00%
	All Other Countries	209	24.8	47.40%	52.60%
	Total	53,813	24	48.90%	51.10%

Source: United States Department of State, United States Department of Homeland Security, United States Department of Health and Human Services (2006). Proposed refugee admissions for fiscal year 2007 - Report to the congress: Submitted on behalf of the president of the United States to the committees on the judiciary United States senate and United States house of representatives in fulfillment of the requirements of section 207(e)(1)-(7) of the Immigration and Nationality Act.

Barriers to Screening, Treatment, and Follow-up Refugees Face

Refugees represent a mass of history, culture, and language. Some come from countries with low literacy rates (Table 2). Providers of care to refugees must keep in mind the newness of being in the U.S., the experiences the refugees have felt, and their beliefs about health and culture (Cochran et al., 2007). Benson (2007) suggests that refugees might only know about HIV, and, therefore, the significance and implications of viral hepatitis might be confusing. In addition, the added stress of caring for a potentially life threatening disease in a country in which they are unfamiliar with might be unbearable. Benson (2007) also states the importance of education through an interpreter through all stages of care to ease stress. However, some interpretations of hepatitis are focused on vocabulary equivalents, which have been shown to be meaningless to some refugees (Jackson et al., 1997). Because of the asymptomatic nature of the illness, refugees might not feel they continue to have the disease because they are not currently experiencing the effects of the illness.

DISCUSSION

Although it can be argued that current refugees underuse health services, it has not been established whether this is associated with cultural barriers, language barriers, reduced perceived needs, reduced needs, or socioeconomic barriers (e.g., lack of access to telephone, transportation to clinic, etc.). Many countries of origin of refugees have much higher rates of hepatitis B and C infections than the U.S. Most refugees carrying hepatitis will be asymptomatic with infection detected by screening. Refugees need counseling, education, and support to come to terms with the implications of hepatitis B and C for both themselves and their families. In the U.S., both viruses can be treated in those with active infection and general practitioners can be involved in diagnosis, follow up, and shared care management.

Currently, hepatitis B and C testing is not required for the refugee application process in the U.S. Preferably, in asymptomatic individuals from high-prevalence regions, hepatitis B screening should be undertaken for either hepatitis B surface antigen carriage, antibody to hepatitis B surface antigen (for immunity), or the antibody to hepatitis B core antigen (for past exposure to the virus). Further hepatitis B testing may be performed depending on the results of the screening tests. Household and sexual contacts of a hepatitis B carrier should be assessed. Those who have not been exposed to hepatitis B or previously immunized should receive a three-dose series of the hepatitis B vaccine. As with all patients, hepatitis C should be considered in immigrants and refugees with any of the following risk factors: any history of injection drugs use; receipt of contaminated blood or blood products; medical or non-medical invasive procedures involving sharing of contaminated equipment; any exposure to hepatitis C; needle-stick or sharp injuries; non-sterile tattooing or body piercing; sharing contaminated personal items (e.g., razors, nail clippers, toothbrush, intranasal equipment for snorting drugs); hepatitis B or HIV infection; undiagnosed liver disease; being a child born to a HCV infected mother; and being a member of a family with intrafamilial type of hepatitis C transmission.

Some immigrants and refugees have very limited opportunity to interface with the health care system and some patients may have cultural sensitivities toward health care workers of the opposite sex. It is important to address social, cultural, and economic factors that may affect treatment adherence. Language barriers may contribute to difficulty in understanding instructions on treatment plans, practice of safer sex, and other preventive measures. In some cultures, it may be difficult to discuss monogamy or condom use. It is important to obtain a history of traditional medicine to prevent toxicities and drug interactions. It is important to address socio-cultural factors that may discourage partner notification. Language barriers may make these health educational interventions more difficult for the healthcare provider. In some cultures, fear of domestic violence may be a reason for reluctance to notify the partner. Clients who receive their first dose of hepatitis B vaccination should be reminded to continue the immunization series.

CONCLUSION

Although overall incidence of hepatitis B in the U.S. is decreasing and incidence of hepatitis C is almost leveled off during the past decade, the trend may not be the same in relation to refugee populations. Refugees make up a small sector of the U.S. population; however, they carry a higher burden of disease from viral hepatitis. Screenings of these diseases are not performed before departure or after arrival. HCV is often asymptomatic and can become chronic. Chronic infection leads to an increased risk of HCC and death. Barriers to health care, including screening, that refugees face are most commonly associated with the cultural gap between their own beliefs and education, and the culture and beliefs of the U.S. The implications of this review indicate a need for the screening of viral hepatitis, immunization of HBV, followed with more comprehensive treatment, and follow-up of care for refugees positive with the infection to decrease the risk of transmission and mortality rates.

REFERENCES

Armstrong, G. L., Wasley, A., Simard, E. P., McQuillan, G. M., Kuhnert, W. L., Alter, M. J. et al. (2006). The prevalence of Hepatitis C virus infection in the United States, 1999 through 2002. *Ann Int Med, 144*, 705-714.

Barnett, E.D. (2004). Infectious disease screening for refugees resettled in the United States. *Travel Medicine, 39*, 833-841.

Benson, J. & Donahue, W. (2007). Hepatitis in refugees who settle in Australia. *Australian Family Practice, 36*(9), 719-725.

Blanchet, E., Defossez, G., Verneau, A., Ingrand, I., Silvain, C., & Beauchant, M. (2003). Epidemiology and management of care of hepatitis C infection in the Poitou-Charentes region in 1997 and 2000. *Gastroentérologie clinique et biologique, 27*(11), 1026-1030.

Bojuwoye, B. J. (1997). The burden of viral hepatitis in Africa. *West African Journal of Medicine, 16*(4), 198-203.

Centers for Disease Control and Prevention. (2009). Surveillance for acute viral hepatitis – United States, 2007. *Morbidity and Mortality Weekly, 58*, 1-32.

Centers for Disease Control and Prevention. (2008). Recommendations for identification and public health management of persons with chronic Hepatitis B virus infection. *MMWR, 57*(RR-8), 1-20.

Centers for Disease Control and Prevention. (1998). Recommendations for prevention and control of hepatitis C virus (HCV) infection and HCV-related chronic disease. *Morbidity and Mortality Weekly Report, 47*(RR-19), 1-39.

Chironna, M., Germinario, C., Lopalco, P.L., Carrozzini, F., Barbuti, S., & Quarto, M. (2002). Prevalence rates of viral hepatitis infection in refugee Kurds from Iraq and Turkey. *Infection, 31*, 70-74.

Cochran, J., O'Fallon, A., & Geltman, P.L. (2007). U.S. medical screening for immigrants and refugees. In: Walker, P. & Barnett, E.D. (Eds.), *Immigrant Medicine* (pp. 123-134). Philadelphia, PA: Saunders Elsevier.

Department of Homeland Security. Refugee arrivals by region and country of nationality: Fiscal years 2000 to 2009 [online]. (2010) [cited 2010 November 18]. Available from: *http://www.dhs.gov/files/statistics/publications/YrBk09RA.shtm.*

Jackson, J.C., Rhodes, L.A., Inui, T.S., & Buchwald, D. (1997). Hepatitis B among the Khmer. *Journal of General Internal Medicine, 12*, 292-298.

Kew, M., Francois, G., Lavanchy, D., Margolis, H., Van Damme, P., Grob, P., Hallauer, J., Shouval, D., Leroux-Roels, G., & Meheus, A. (2004). Prevention of hepatitis c virus infection. *Journal of Viral Hepatitis, 11*, 198-205.

Lauer, G.M., & Walker, B.D. (2001). Hepatitis C virus infection. *New England Journal of Medicine, 345*(1), 41-52.

Lifson, A.R., Thai, D., O'Fallon, A., Mills, W.A., & Hang, K. (2002). Prevalence of tuberculosis, hepatitis B virus, and intestinal parasitic infections among refugees to Minnesota. *Public Health Reports, 117*, 69-77.

Manos, M.M., Leyden, W. A., Murphy, R. C., Terrault, N. A., & Bell, B. P. (2008). Limitations of conventionally derived chronic liver disease mortality rates: results of a comprehensive assessment. *Hepatology, 47*, 1150-7.

McCarthy, M.C., El-Tigani, A., Khalid, I.O., & Hyams, K.C. (1994). Hepatitis B and C in Juba, southern Sudan: Results of a serosurvey. *Transactions of the Royal Society of Tropical Medicine and Hygiene, 88*, 534-536.

McQuillan, G.M., Coleman, P. J., Kruszon-Moran, D., Moyer, L. A., Lambert, S. B., & Margolis, H. S.(1999). Prevalence of Hepatitis B virus infection in the United States: The National Health and Nutrition Examination Surveys, 1976 through 1994. *AJPH, 89*(1), 14-18.

Museru, O. & Franco-Paredes, C. (2009). Epidemiology and clinical outcomes of hepatitis B virus infection among refugees seen at a U.S. travel medicine clinic: 2005-2008. *Travel Medicine and Infectious Disease, 7*, 171-174.

Museru, O.I., Vargas, M., Kinyua, M., Alexander, K.T., Franco-Paredes, C. & Oladele, A. (2010). Hepatitis B virus infection among refugees resettled in the U.S.: High prevalence and challenges in access to health care. *Journal of Immigrant Minority Health, 12*, 823-827.

Nafeh, M.A., Medhat, A., Shehata, M., Mikhail, N.N.H., Swifee, Y., Abdel-Hamid, M., Watts, S., Fix, A.D., Strickland, G.T., Anwar, W., & Sallam, I. (2000). Hepatitis C in a community in upper Egypt: I. cross-sectional survey. *American Journal of Tropical Hygeine, 63*, 236-241.

Poustschi, H., Sepanlou, S.G., Esmaili, S., Mehrabi, N., & Ansarymoghadam, A. (2010). Hepatocellular carcinoma in the world and the Middle East. *Middle East Journal of Digestive Diseases, 2*(1), 31-41.

Roussos, A., Goritsas, C., Pappas, T., Spanaki, M., Papdaki, P., & Ferti, A. (2003). Prevalence of hepatitis B and C markers among refugees in Athens. *World Journal of Gastroenterology, 9*(5), 993-995.

Tarfuri, S., Prato, R., Martinelli, D., Melpignano, L., De Palma, M., & Quarto, M. (2010). Prevalence of hepatitis B, C, HIV and syphilis markers among refugees in Bari, Italy. *BMC Infectious Diseases, 10*(213), 1-15.

Udeagu Pratt, C.N., Paone, D., Carter, R.J., & Layton, M.C. (2002). Hepatitis C screening and management practices: A survey of drug treatment and syringe exchange program in New York City. *American Journal of Public Health, 92*(8), 1254-1256.

United Nations High Commissioner for Refugees. UNHCR country operations profile – Egypt [online]. (2010) [cited 2010 December 2]. Available from: *http://www.unhcr.org/cgi-bin/texis/vtx/page?page=49e486356.*

United States Department of State. Form DS-2053, Medical examination for immigrant or refugee applicant [online]. (1991) [cited 2010 November 17]. Available from: *http://photos.state.gov/libraries/vietnam/8621/pdf-forms/DS-2053.pdf.*

Vassilev, Z.P., Strauss, S.M., Astone, J., & Des Jarlais, D.C. (2004). Injection drug users and the provision of hepatitis C-related services in a nationwide sample of drug treatment programs. *The Journal of Behavioral Health Services & Research, 31*(2), 208-216.

Vogt, T.M., Wise, M. E., Shih, H., & Williams, I. T. l. (2007). Hepatitis B mortality in the United States, 1990–2004. *Paper presented at 45th Annual Meeting of the Infectious Disease Society of America; October 4–7, San Diego, CA.*

Wise, M., Bialek, S., Finelli, L., Bell, B. P., & Sorvillo, F. l. (2008). Changing trends in Hepatitis C-related mortality in the United States, 1995–2004. *Hepatology, 47,* 1–8.

World Health Organization. Viral hepatitis: Report by the Secretariat [online]. World Health Assembly, A63(15), 1-6. (2005) [cited 2010 December 1]. Available from: *http://apps.who.int/gb/ebwha/pdf_files/WHA63/A63_15-en.pdf.*

World Health Organization. (1999). Global surveillance and control of hepatitis C. Report of a WHO consultation organized in collaboration with the viral hepatitis control board, Antwerp, Belgium. *Journal of Viral Hepatitis, 6,* 35-47.

World Health Organization. Hepatitis B (HepB3) immunization coverage among 1-year-olds (%). [online]. (2010). [cited 2010 November 17].

Available from: *http://apps.who.int/*immunization_monitoring/en/globalsummary/timeseries/tscoveragehepb3.htm.

Xu, J., Kochanek, K.D., Murphy, S.L., & Tejada-Vera, B. (2010). Deaths: Final data for 2007. *National Vital Statistics Report, 58*(19), 1-136.

Vassilev, Z. P., Strauss, S. M., Astone, J., & Des Jarlais, D.C. (2004) Injection drug users and the provision of hepatitis C-related services in a nationwide sample of drug treatment programs. *The Journal of Behavioral Health Services & Research*, 31(2),208-216.

In: Contemporary Issues in Public Health
Editors: S.G. Obeng, A. Youssefagha et al.
ISBN: 978-1-63117-933-4
© 2014 Nova Science Publishers, Inc.

Chapter 4

PREDICTION OF TOTAL WATER REQUIREMENTS FOR AGRICULTURE IN THE ARAB WORLD UNDER CLIMATE CHANGE

Gamal El Afandi[1], Samiha Ouda[2], Fouad Khalil[2] and Sayed Abd El-Hafez[2]

[1]Tuskegee University, AL, US
[2]Water Requirements and Field Irrigation Research Department Soils, Water, and, Environment Research Institute, Egypt

ABSTRACT

This paper aimed at determining the percentage increase in the required water for agriculture in all Arab countries under the expected climate change in 2025. Data was gathered from the Arabic Center for Dry and Arid Zones Studies. Descriptive statistics were done for the mean temperature values to determine the mean value of each year and the mean for100 years. Furthermore, the temperature range was also calculated for a100 year period. Results of the study showed that by 2025 the demand for irrigation water will increase in all the Arab countries. Also, the Arab countries could be divided into three groups according to the temperature range: countries where the range was identified as being less than 2.0 °C (e.g., Egypt); countries where the temperature range was anticipated to be between 2.0 to 2.6°C (e.g., Algeria); and countries where the range of temperature was expected to be higher than 2.6°C (e.g., Bahrain). The above situation will create a problem in allocation of water resources between different sectors. In order to conserve water, avoid the wasteful use of water resources, and avoid catastrophe, the authors recommend the use of adaptation measures.

INTRODUCTION

Most of the Arab countries are located in arid and semi-arid zones known for their scanty annual rainfall, very high rates of evaporation, and, consequently, extremely insufficient renewable water resources. The per capita water share of renewable water resources in the Arab Region is less than 10% of the global average (Al-Weshah, 2008). Sustainable management of water resources is a must, as water scarcity is becoming more and more a constraint impeding the social and economic development of many countries in the region (AbuZeid & AbdelMegeed, 2004).

The Arabic region is considered one of the most vulnerable regions to climate change impacts, on account of its water scarcity, which is the highest in the world (Elasha, 2010). Giorgi (2006) identifies North Africa and the Mediterranean among the most physically sensitive regions to climate change. Climate models are projecting hotter, drier, and less predictable climate, resulting in a drop in water run-off by 20% to 30% in most of the region by 2050, mainly due to rising temperatures and lower precipitation (Milly, 2005), in addition to an increase in the frequency and intensity of extreme weather events, such as, droughts and floods (El-Quesy, 2009). The fragile water situation in the region is more sensitive to climate change that may cause economic, social, and environmental effects. One of the major drawbacks of research in and on the Arab region is data availability: regular measurements, continuous monitoring, and neutral evaluation of the water status in the area is either missing or only available in isolated surveys that might be separated by long time spans with unavailable records. This adds to the uncertainty of the effect of climate change on water resources in most of the Arab countries (El-Quesy, 2009), which in turn will affect the future of agriculture.

In Arab countries, the agricultural sector consumes over 83% of the water in the region, and 37% of an economically active population of 126 million were engaged in agriculture in 2006 (IFAD, 2009). Because agriculture is an activity developed under climatic condition, the impacts of climate change could affect a large segment of the population. Furthermore, agriculture is under pressure to produce more food to help reduce the Arab countries' enormous food imports bill, which is equivalent to US$ 28 billion in 2006

(UNDP, 2008). Previous research was done in Egypt on the effect of climate change on water requirements for crops. It revealed that it would increase by 16% for summer crops compared to their current requirements under current conditions. Furthermore, climate change conditions could decrease water demand for winter crops up to 2% in the year of 2050 (Eid & El-Mowelhi, 1998). In this context, management of water supply and water demand are equally critical. In order to ensure long-term adaptation to climate change and scarcer water availability, new approaches and policy frameworks, together with innovative solutions, are essential (IFAD, 2009).

Therefore, it is important to determine how the amount of water required to support agriculture in the Arab countries will be affected by climate change conditions. It is expected that the required water for agriculture will increase under climate change condition as a direct effect of increasing evapotranspiration of the growing crops (Gardner, Pearce, & Mitchell, 1985). The quantification of that effect is hard to do using modeling techniques in each country as a result of the lack of trained staff. However, a simpler, yet accurate, procedure could be used to do the assessment, i.e., prediction equations resulted from regression analysis (Draper & Smith, 1987).

The objective of this paper was to determine the percentage of increase in the required water for agriculture in all Arabic countries under the expected climate change in 2025.

MATERIALS AND METHODS

Source of Data

Required water for agriculture for 21 Arabic countries was obtained from a report prepared by "The Arab Center for the Studies of Arid Zones and Dry Lands (ACSAD)" in 1997. In this report, agricultural water requirements for each Arabic country were predicted in 2010 and 2025. Furthermore, mean temperature data in centigrade was obtained from the "Climatic Research Unit" in the United Kingdom from the following web site: http://www.cru. uea.ac.uk/~timm/cty/obs/TYNCY11.html. The data were values of mean temperature in a period of 100 years from 1901-2000.

Data on area, population, total renewable water resources, and water withdrawal for agriculture for each Arabic country was obtained from AQUASTAT. AQUASTAT is Food and Agriculture Organization's (FAO) global water information system, developed by the Land and Water Division.

The main mandate of the program is to collect, analyze, and disseminate information on water resources, water uses, and agricultural water management worldwide. The main mandate of the programme is to collect, analyze and disseminate information on water resources, water uses, and agricultural water management, with an emphasis on countries in Africa, Asia, Latin America and the Caribbean. This allows interested users to find comprehensive and regularly updated information at global, regional, and national levels http://www.fao.org/nr/water/aquastat/main/index.stm.

Statistical Analysis

Descriptive statistics were done for the mean temperature values to determine the mean value of each year and the mean of the 100 years. Furthermore, the temperature range, which is the difference between the highest and lowest value of yearly mean of temperature was calculated for the 100 years (Snedicor & Cochran, 1980). The Arabic countries were classified according to temperature range into three groups to be used as an indication of the vulnerability of these countries to climate change.

Multiple linear regressions (Draper & Smith, 1987) was used to fit a line through the set of observations, and test how the value of irrigation water requirements for agriculture in each country is affected by the value of its annual mean temperature. As a result, a prediction equation, coefficient of determination (R^2), and standard error of estimates (SE %) were obtained. The coefficient of determination is the amount of variability due to all independent variables, and the standard error of estimates is a measurement of precision, i.e., the closeness of predicted and observed value to each other.

Both irrigation water quantities in 2025 and annual mean temperature values of each country were used to develop a regression equation to predict the value of irrigation water required for agriculture under climate change. The amount required in 2010 was used as a base amount to determine the percentage of increase in 2025. The accuracy of these equations in predicting water required for agriculture in each country was judged by several parameters, i.e., high value of R^2, low value of SE%, the significance of the regression in the ANOVA table, the significance of regression coefficient for mean temperature (MTemp), and the regression coefficient for mean temperature lies within confidence interval.

PREDICTION OF TOTAL WATER REQUIREMENTS FOR AGRICULTURE UNDER CLIMATE CHANGE

The developed prediction equations were used to predict the required amount of irrigation water for agriculture in 2025. The IPCC report (2001) estimates an increase in temperature in the Arab region of up to 2°C in the next 15-20 years. Thus, 2.0°C was added to mean temperature to represent the change in climate in 2025 and irrigation water required for agriculture was predicted in each country using its developed prediction equation.

RESULTS AND DISCUSSION

Brief Description of the Arab Countries

The Arabic countries are divided into four geographic regions: The Eastern Arabic region, the Arabic Island region, the Middle Arabic and the Western Arabic region (Figure 1 and Table 1).

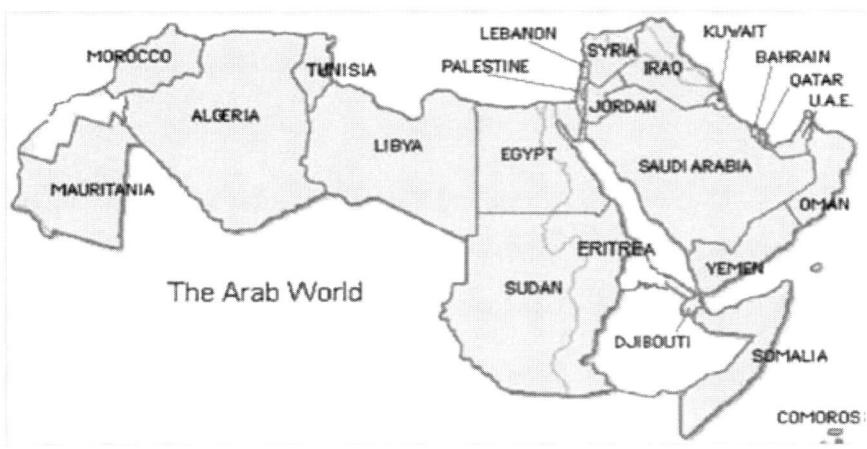

Source: Arab Bay.com, http://www.arabbay.com/arabmap.htm.

Figure 1. Map of the Arabic countries.

The Eastern Arabic Region
This region is located east of the Mediterranean Sea in Asia. Five countries are included in it: Jordan, Syria, Iraq, Occupied Palestine, and

Lebanon. Iraq has the largest area and the largest population, with water withdrawal percentage for agriculture equal 79%. The highest amount of total renewable water resources exists in Lebanon, 60% of it is withdrawal for agriculture. Syria has the largest water withdrawal percentage for agriculture at 88%.

Table 1. Total Area, Population, and Total Renewable Water in the Eastern Arabic Region in 2005

Arab Countries	Area (km²)	Population (10⁶ inhabitant)	TRWR (10⁶ m³/year)	% WWA
Jordan	88,780	5.7	682	65
Syria	185,180	19.0	4300	88
Iraq	438,320	28.8	3520	79
Occupied Palestine	6,020	3.7	837	45
Lebanon	10,400	3.6	4800	60

TRWR= total renewable water resources; % WWA= % of water withdrawal for agriculture

The Arabic Island Region

This region is composed of 7 countries located in Asia between east of the Red Sea and the Arabic Gulf (Figure 1 and Table 2). Saudi Arabia has the largest area, the largest population and the largest total renewable water resources. Yemen has the highest percentage of water withdrawal for agriculture.

Table 2. Total Area, Population, and Total Renewable Water Resources in the Arabic Island Region in 2005

Arab Countries	Area (km²)	Population (10⁶ inhabitant)	TRWR (10⁶ m³/year)	% WWA
United Arab Emirates	83,600	4.5	150	83
Bahrain	710	0.7	4.0	45**
Saudi Arabia	2,150,000	24.6	4200	88
Oman	309,500	2.6	1400	88
Qatar	11,000	0.8	58.1	59
Kuwait	17,820	2.7	20*	44
Yemen	527,970	21.0	2100	90

TRWR= total renewable water resources; % WWA= % of water withdrawal for agriculture. * Ground water inflow. ** The value for Abu Dhabi Emirate only.

Middle Arabic Region

This region is located in the Northeast of Africa and composed of 4 countries: Djibouti, Sudan, Somalia, and Egypt. Sudan has the largest area and the largest total renewable water resources. Sudan and Somalia have the highest percentage of water withdrawal for agriculture at 99%.

Table 3. Total Area, Population, and Total Renewable Water Resources in the Middle Arabic Region in 2004

Arab Countries	Area (km^2)	Population (10^6 inhabitant)	TRWR (10^6 m^3/year)	% WWA
Djibouti	23,200	0.7	300	13
Sudan	2,500,000	34.3	149000	99
Somalia	637,660	6.8	1420	99
Egypt	1,000,000	73.4	5730	86

TRWR= total renewable water resources; % WWA= % of water withdrawal for agriculture.

The Western Arabic Region

The five Arabic countries in this region are in the Northwestern part of Africa. These countries are: Tunisia, Algeria, Libya, Morocco, and Mauritania. The largest area was found for Algeria, which also has the largest population. The largest total renewable water resources exist in Morocco. Moreover, the highest percentage of water withdrawal for agriculture is observed in Mauritania.

Table 4. Total Area, Population, and Total Renewable Water Resources in the Western Arabic Region in 2004

Arab Countries	Area (km^2)	Population (10^6 inhabitant)	TRWR (10^6 m^3/year)	% WWA
Tunisia	163,610	9.9	4600	82
Algeria	2,400,000	32.3	11300	65
Libya	1,760,000	5.7	200	83
Morocco	446,550	31.0	29000	87
Mauritania	1,025,520	3.0	11100	88

TRWR= total renewable water resources; % WWA= % of water withdrawal for agriculture.

A common trend existed in the Arabic countries, which is irrigation water withdrawal normally far exceeds the consumptive use of irrigation because water lost in its distribution from its source to the crops (FAO-AQUASTAT). Therefore, improving conveyance efficiency could play an important role in reducing irrigation water losses, especially under the relatively high percentage of water withdrawal for agriculture in most of the Arabic countries.

Vulnerability of the Arabic Countries to the Impact of Climate Change

Vulnerability is the degree to which a system is susceptible to or unable to cope with adverse effects of climate change, including climate variability and extremes (IPCC, 2001). The range of the annual mean temperature over the studied period (1901-2000) was used to classify the Arabic countries into three groups to determine its vulnerability to climate change.

Vulnerable Arabic Countries

There are 10 countries in this group, all of them located in Asia, where temperature range over 100 years is higher than 2.6°C. This result implies that these countries are more vulnerable to climate change (see Table 5), compared with the rest of the Arab countries. Figure (2) showed that all the Asian Arabic countries experience a rise in temperature around 2°C in the period of 1974-2004, except for Yemen and Oman.

Table 5. Vulnerable Arabic Countries to Climate Change According to Temperature Range in the Period between 1901-2000

Arab Countries	Mean Temperature average of 100 years (°C)	Temperature range over 100 years (°C)
Jordan	18.2	3.0
Iraq	21.3	2.9
Lebanon	16.3	2.9
United Arab Emirates	26.8	2.7
Saudi Arabia	24.6	2.9
Kuwait	25.2	2.8
Occupied Palestine	19.1	3.1
Syria	17.7	3.1
Qatar	27.0	3.3
Bahrain	27.0	3.6

Mean temperature in this group was between 16.3-27.0°C. The highest mean temperature was observed in Bahrain at 27.0°C, which also has the highest range in this group at 3.6°C. The lowest mean temperature existed in Lebanon, where it was 16.3°C. However, its temperature range was relatively high 2.9°C (see Table 5).

Arabic Countries with Intermediate Vulnerability

Temperature range over 100 years in this group was between 2.0 and 2.5°C (see Table 6). This group contains 4 countries located in the Northwest of Africa, i.e., Algeria, Mauritania, Morocco, and Tunisia. These countries are also vulnerable to climate change as shown in Figure (2).

Regarding mean temperature, it was between 17.1-27.5°C. The lowest mean temperature was found in Morocco at 17.1°C, with a temperature range equal 2.4°C. The highest mean temperature was observed in Mauritania, where it was 27.5°C and the temperature range was 2.5°C (see Table 6).

Table 6. Intermediate Vulnerable Arabic Countries to Climate Change According to Temperature Range in the Period between 1901-2000

Arab Countries	Mean Temperature average of 100 years (°C)	Temperature range over 100 years (°C)
Algeria	22.4	2.0
Morocco	17.1	2.4
Tunisia	19.0	2.5
Mauritania	27.5	2.5

Table 7. Less Vulnerable Arabic Countries to Climate Change According to Temperature Range in the Period between 1901-2000

Arab Countries	Mean Temperature average of 100 years (°C)	Temperature range over 100 years (°C)
Somalia	27.1	1.4
Yemen	23.7	1.6
Libya	21.9	1.6
Djibouti	28.7	1.7
Oman	25.4	1.7
Sudan	26.8	1.9
Egypt	22.3	1.9

Less Vulnerable Arabic Countries

All the countries in this group are located in the Northeast and East of Africa, except Yemen and Oman. Temperature range was less than 2.0°C (see Table 7). Figure (2) showed that these countries are less vulnerable to climate change.

In this group, mean temperature was between 21.9-28.7°C. Djibouti has the highest mean temperature equal to 28.7°C and its temperature range was 1.7°C; whereas, Libya has the lowest mean temperature equal to 21.9°C, with temperature range equal to 1.6°C (see Table 7).

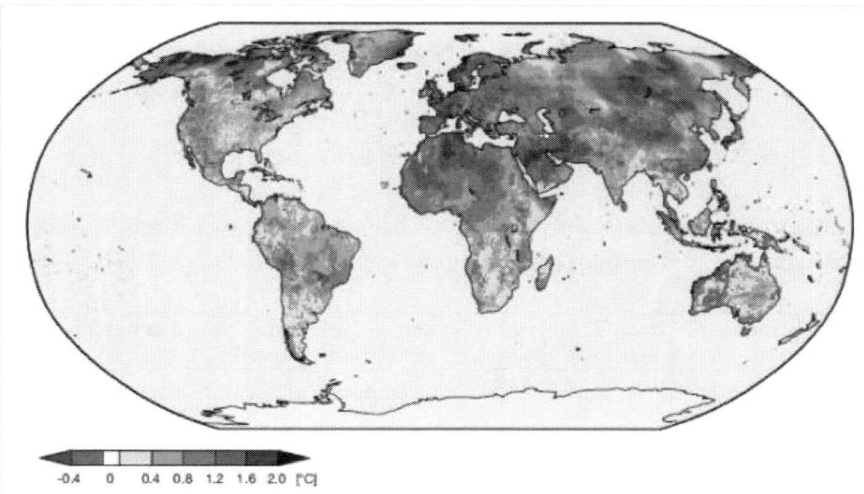

Source: WBGU1, data Potsdam Institute for Climate Impact Research (PIK) climate database

Figure 2. Linear temperature trends for the period 1974-2004.

The Developed Prediction Equations

Prediction equations, coefficient of determination, standard error of estimates, in addition to confidence interval for regression coefficient of mean temperature are included in Table (8) for vulnerable Arabic countries. Results in Table (8) imply that the developed prediction equations could predict the amount of required irrigation water for agriculture with a high degree of accuracy as a result of high value of R^2, low value of SE%, the significance of regression coefficient for mean temperature (MTemp), and that the regression coefficient for mean temperature lies within the confidence interval.

Table 8. Prediction equation, Coefficient of Determination, and Standard Error of Estimates for Vulnerable Arabic Countries

Arab Countries	Prediction equations	R^2	SE%	CI (95%)
Jordan	Y^= 8837.50 + 20.14(MTemp)**	0.86	0.05	21.77-18.51
Iraq	Y^= 48499.47 + 47.64(MTemp)**	0.92	0.02	44.79-50.48
Lebanon	Y^= 3948.29 + 45.69(MTemp)**	0.93	0.02	43.15-48.22
United Arab Emirates	Y^= 984.11 + 60.14(MTemp)**	0.93	0.32	56.48-63.80
Saudi Arabia	Y^= 26496.04 + 60.13(MTemp)**	0.91	0.04	56.26-64.00
Kuwait	Y^= 2809.42 + 53.60(MTemp)**	0.92	0.19	50.53-56.67
Palestine	Y^= 3921.35 + 45.78(MTemp)**	0.92	0.02	43.08-48.47
Syria	Y^= 38422.37 + 44.74(MTemp)**	0.93	0.02	42.26-47.22
Qatar	Y^= 673.4 + 49.83(MTemp)**	0.91	1.34	46.57-53.09
Bahrain	Y^= -517.44 + 45.47(MTemp)**	0.89	1.32	42.34-48.60

Y^= amount of required water for agriculture ($10^6 m^3$); MTemp= mean temperature from 1901-2000 (°C); R^2= coefficient of determination; SE%= standard error of estimates; CI= confidence interval for regression coefficient of mean temperature at 95% level of significant.

Furthermore, similar situation was observed for the prediction equations for Arabic countries with intermediate vulnerability to climate change and less vulnerable Arabic countries for climate change in Table (9) and (10), respectively.

Table 9. Prediction Equation, Coefficient of Determination, and Standard Error of Estimates for Arabic Countries with Intermediate Vulnerability

Arab countries	Prediction equations	R^2	SE%	CI (95%)
Algeria	Y^= 48621.16 + 59.49(MTemp)**	0.95	0.01	56.76-62.22
Morocco	Y^= 40123.22 + 60.29(MTemp)**	0.93	0.02	56.97-63.61
Tunisia	Y^= 1788.24 + 58.23(Mtemp)**	0.92	0.24	46.34-51.57
Mauritania	Y^= 1788.24 + 58.23(Mtemp)**	0.92	0.24	54.82-61.63

Y^= amount of required water for agriculture ($10^6 m^3$); MTemp= mean temperature from 1901-2000 (°C); R^2= coefficient of determination; SE%= standard error of estimates; CI= confidence interval for regression coefficient of mean temperature at 95% level of significant.

Table 10. Prediction Equation, Coefficient of Determination, and Standard Error of Estimates for Less Vulnerable Arabic Countries

Arab countries	Prediction equations	R^2	SE%	CI (95%)
Somalia	Y^= 11767.89+110.49(MTemp)**	0.87	0.07	101.82-119.16
Yemen	Y^= 16894.33+ 93.92(MTemp)**	0.87	0.05	86.93-100.91
Libya	Y^= 9582.92 + 76.15(MTemp)**	0.96	0.05	93.21-79.08
Djibouti	Y^= -1574.63 + 89.78(MTemp)**	0.92	0.81	84.47-95.05
Oman	Y^= 228.52 + 96.14(MTemp)**	0.91	0.32	90.04-102.24
Sudan	Y^= 54076 + 61.86(MTemp)**	0.97	0.00	59.69-64.03
Egypt	Y^= 125369 + 63.60(MTemp)**	0.97	0.00	61.35-65.86

Y^= amount of required water for agriculture ($10^6 m^3$); MTemp= mean temperature from 1901-2000 (°C); R^2= coefficient of determination; SE%= standard error of estimates; CI= confidence interval for regression coefficient of mean temperature at 95% level of significant.

Prediction of the Effect of Climate Change on Required Water for Agriculture

Vulnerable Arabic Countries

Table 11. Predicted Total Required Water Amount for Agriculture in 2010 Under Current Climate and in 2025 under Temperature Increase by 2°C for Vulnerable Arabic Countries

Arab Countries	Amount in 2010 ($10^6 m^3$)	Amount in 2025 ($10^6 m^3$)	Percent increase in the amount in 2025
Lebanon	4246	4787	12.74%
Qatar	589	722	22.58%
Iraq	40198	49652	23.52%
Jordan	7266	9244	27.22%
Bahrain	619	801	29.40%
Palestine	3900	5289	35.62%
Syria	29135	39304	34.90%
United Arab Emirates	1929	2716	40.80%
Saudi Arabia	19649	28126	43.14%
Kuwait	2881	3691	28.12%
Average	11041	14433	30.72%

The amount of required water for agriculture in 2025 under 2 °C increases in temperature for the group of vulnerable Arabic countries is expected to increase by an average of 30.72%. The highest percentage of increase is expected to be in Saudi Arabia, where the value is 43.14% (see Table 11). This high percentage could be explained by the fact that the per capita water consumption in Saudi Arabia is high (FAO-AQUASTAT).

In contrast, the lowest percentage is projected to be in Lebanon at 12.74% (see Table 11). In Lebanon, the share of water withdrawal for agriculture is likely to decrease over the coming years as more water will have to be diverted for municipal and industrial purposes (FAO-AQUASTAT).

Arabic Countries with Intermediate Vulnerability

The predicted amount of required water for agriculture in 2025 under 2 °C increases in temperature for this group is ranged between 10-24%, with an average of 18.12% (see Table 12). Algeria will have the highest percentage of required water amount for agriculture, i.e., 24.12%, where it has the largest total area in this group (see Table 4).

On the contrary, Tunisia will have the lowest percentage equal to 10.12% (Table 12), where it has the smallest total area (see Table 4).

Table 12. Predicted Total Required Water Amount for Agriculture in 2010 under Current Climate and in 2025 under Temperature Increase by 2°C for Arabic Countries with Intermediate Vulnerability

Arab Countries	Amount in 2010 ($10^6 m^3$)	Amount in 2025 ($10^6 m^3$)	Percent increase in the amount in 2025
Tunisia	10932	12038	10.12%
Mauritania	3073	3506	14.09%
Morocco	35830	41275	15.20%
Algeria	40343	50073	24.12%
Average	18438	21783	18.14%

Less Vulnerable Arabic Countries

The highest percentage of required water amount for agriculture for this group in 2025 under 2°C increases in temperature will occur in Egypt, where the percentage will be 57.39% (see Table 13). This high percentage could be explained by the high percentage of water withdrawal for agriculture, which is 86% (see Table 4). Furthermore, the high population growth rate estimated by

1.8 (FAO-AQUASTAT) put pressure on the agricultural sector to produce more food to attain food security.

Sudan will have the lowest percentage of required water amount for agriculture at 20.89% (see Table 13) as a result of low population density, which is 14 inhabitant/ km^2 (FAO-AQUASTAT).

Table 13. Predicted Total Required Water Amount for Agriculture in 2010 under Current Climate and in 2025 Under Temperature Increase by 2°C for Less Vulnerable Arabic Countries

Arab Countries	Amount in 2010 (10^6m^3)	Amount in 2025 (10^6m^3)	Percent increase in the amount in 2025
Sudan	46207	55858	20.89%
Somalia	12246	14983	22.35%
Yemen	16780	22567	34.49%
Djibouti	1051	1303	23.98%
Oman	2170	2863	31.94%
Libya	8308	11403	37.25%
Egypt	80636	126915	57.39%
Average	23914	33699	40.92%

CONCLUSION

The majority of Arab countries is considered among the highest in water scarcity in the World, and in many places demand for water already exceeds supply. Higher temperatures and less rainfall will reduce the flow of rivers and streams, slow the rate at which aquifers recharge, and make the entire region more arid. The presented data showed that in 12 countries of 21 Arabic countries, the percentage of water withdrawal for agriculture was higher than 80% (see Tables 5, 6, and 7). These previous changes will have a series of effects, particularly on agriculture, energy, and food security.

Climate change is expected to affect food security through its impact on agriculture and food production systems. According to the IPCC (2007), by the 2080s, agricultural potential in the developing world could fall by 9% under climate change condition. A study by the World Bank (2007) concluded that, under climate change, for the Arabic region as a whole, agricultural output will decrease 21% in value terms by 2080, with peaks of an almost 40% decrease in countries like Algeria and Morocco.

The approach developed in this study relies both on the countries' statistics, temperature, and modeling to provide a more reliable database for each Arabic country. Thus, the developed prediction equation could be a very important tool to assess the impact of increasing temperature on the amount of water assigned for agriculture. Our results showed that under temperature increase by 2°C, the total required water for agriculture in the Arabic countries would be increased by a percentage between 9% and 36%. The large variation in the previous percentage is mainly due to population growth and increasing demand for water assigned for agriculture. As a result, in 2025, the demand for irrigation water will increase in all the Arab countries and will create a problem in allocation of water resources between different sectors. The availability of such information will increase the ability of the policy makers in each Arabic country to prepare the appropriate developmental plans.

The Arab governments need to use adaptation measures to conserve water and avoid the wasteful use of water resources. Improving irrigation efficiency in Arabic countries using surface irrigation and improving agricultural practices techniques could help in preserving irrigation water. Similarly, improving water harvesting techniques in Arabic countries using rain fed irrigation could also an important procedure to sustain water resources.

REFERENCES

AbuZeid, K. & AbdelMegeed, A. (2004). Status of integrated water resources management planning in Arab Mediterranean Countries. *IWRM, International Water Demand Management Conference*, Dead Sea, Jordan.

Al-Weshah R. A, (2008) "Sustainable Water Resources Management in the Arab World" *ISESCO Journal of Sciences and Technology*. Vol. 4 No. 5, 48-54.

Arab Center for the Studies of Arid Zones and Dry Lands (ACSAD) 1997: *Available water resources in the Arab world and their adequacy to the requirements of economic and social development*.

Draper, N. R. & Smith, H. (1987). *Applied regression analysis*. John Wiley and Sons, Inc. New York. pp. 397 - 402.

Eid, H.M. & El-Mowelhi, N.M. (1998). Impact of climate change on field crops and water needs in Egypt. *African International Environmental Conference*. October, 1998, Egypt.

Elasha, B.O. (2010). Mapping of climate change threats and human development impacts in Arab region. Arab Human Development Report. UNDP.

El-Quasy, D., 2009. Impact of climate change: vulnerability and adaptation on fresh water. In (Ed.) Tolba, M.K and Saab, N.W., Impact of climate change on Arab countries. *Arab Forum for Environment and Development* 75-86.

Gardner, F. P., Pearce, R.B., & Mitchell, R.L. (1985). *Physiology of crop plants*. Iowa State University Press. Ames, Iowa.

Giorgi, F., (2006). Climate change Hot-Spots. *Geophysical Research Letters* 33 (L08707). doi:10.1029/2006GL025734.

In J. J. McCarthy, O. F. Canziani, N. A. Leary, D. J. Dokken and K. S. White, eds. Cambridge, UK: *Cambridge University Press*. 1000 pp.

Intergovernmental Panel on Climate Change IPCC. 2001. *Climate Change 2001: Impacts, Adaptation & Vulnerability: Contribution of Working Group II to the Third Assessment Report of the IPCC.*

International Fund for Agricultural Development (IFAD). (2009). *Fighting water scarcity in the Arab countries.*

IPCC 2007. Climate Change 2007: Impacts, Adaptation and Vulnerability. Contribution of Working Group II to the Fourth Assessment Report of the IPCC. In M.L. Parry, O.F. Canziani, J.P. Palutikof, P.J. van der Linden and C.E.Hanson, eds. *Cambridge University Press*, Cambridge, UK, 976pp.

Milly, E.A. (2005). Global pattern of trends in stream flow and water availability in a changing climate. *Nature*, 438(17) 347-350.

Sendicor, G.W. & Cochran, W.G. (1980). *Statistical Method. 7th Edition*. Iowa State University Press. Ames, Iowa.

UNITED NATIONS DEVELOPMENT PROGRAM (UNDP) (2008). *Food security, poverty, and agriculture in Arab countries: Facts, challenges, and policy considerations.*

World Bank. (2007). Middle East and North Africa Region (MENA) Sustainable Development Sector Department (MNSSD) *Regional Business Strategy to Address Climate Change Preliminary draft for consultation and feedback.*

In: Contemporary Issues in Public Health
Editors: S.G. Obeng, A. Youssefagha et al.
ISBN: 978-1-63117-933-4
© 2014 Nova Science Publishers, Inc.

Chapter 5

ROLE OF INFRASTRUCTURE DEVELOPMENT AND PREVENTION IN COMBAT AGAINST HIV/AIDS IN AFRICA: OPPORTUNITIES BEING LOST

Wasantha Jayawardene, Ahmed Youssefagha, Susan Middlestadt, David Lohrmann and Mohamed Torabi
Indiana University, US

ABSTRACT

This review consists of 73 studies from five databases. The studies selected fall under social/physical infrastructure and prevention. Inconsistent use of condoms, having multiple sex partners, not worrying about sexually transmitted infections, having a sex partner who had not been tested for HIV, and not revealing HIV status to a partner are found to be common problems. Poverty, food insecurity, low education, social injustice, and violence play major roles in the HIV epidemic worsening in Africa. Women and urban populations have a higher risk. Infrastructure deficiencies, discrimination, sexual violence, and human rights violations are prominent. HIV infection among pregnant women and adolescents remains a significant issue. Therefore, current interventions on infrastructure development, social networks improvement, and prevention should be revised.

INTRODUCTION

HIV/AIDS remains one of the major challenges to public health, especially in Africa. More than 33 million people are living with HIV/AIDS globally. Of these, two-thirds live in countries south of the Sahara according to December 2007 estimates (WHO, 2008). Additionally, over two-thirds of the estimated 2.5 million new infections in 2007 occurred in this region. More than three quarters (1.6 million) of AIDS deaths are among people of this African region. It is now evident that, with increased and concerted efforts, the HIV/AIDS epidemic in Africa can be controlled. Available data suggest that the epidemic curve has leveled off in some countries while it is beginning to do so in other countries. More than half the countries in Africa have an HIV prevalence of less than 4% among pregnant women attending antenatal care (ANC) clinics. Many countries are observing a decline in HIV infection trends among pregnant women attending ANC clinics. Countries such as Benin, Nigeria, Côte d'Ivoire, Burkina Faso, Burundi, Kenya, Ethiopia, Uganda, Rwanda, and Zimbabwe have observed a decline in the prevalence of HIV infection (WHO, 2008). Available data on HIV prevalence clearly show that Africa does not have a homogenous epidemic. Marked diversity in HIV prevalence levels exists among regions and countries as well as within countries. Gender differences in the epidemic remain prominent, with women being infected more often than men. Differences are more marked within young age groups where more than thrice as many young women aged 15–24 years are affected compared with male contemporaries. Diversity of the epidemic and gender differences must be taken into consideration when planning and implanting HIV interventions.

METHODS

A literature review was conducted using scientific articles from five databases: Medline, Academic Search Premier, Africa-Wide Information, CINAHL Plus, and MLA. In the initial phase, 127 articles published between 2000 and 2010, inclusive of both years, were selected under the topic "HIV/AIDS in African continent." This selection included several categories of research articles: descriptive, analytical, observational, experimental, and literature reviews. The majority of the studies were descriptive and cross-sectional in design. In phase two, 73 studies were selected based on content:

information related to (1) social and physical infrastructure; and (2) prevention in relation to the HIV/AIDS epidemic in Africa. To keep a balance between all three areas discussed in the review, approximately equal numbers of studies representing each topic were selected. All the important aspects of the emerging HIV epidemic on the African continent were addressed.

DISCUSSION

Social and Physical Infrastructure

Addressing HIV/AIDS causes an increase in economic growth by counterbalancing population pressure and poverty. Incentives to mitigate HIV/AIDS lie in both infected households and uninfected households, so an urgent need exists for policies to curtail the economic costs (Thurlow, Gow, & George, 2009). Empirical evidence has demonstrated the pathways through which HIV/AIDS undermines income and raises the vulnerability of livelihood collapse. But little attention has been paid to the livelihood strategies that create risky social interactions that raise the chance of contracting HIV (Masanjala, 2007).

Cash transfer programs already reach millions of people in Africa and have large impacts on the population's education, health, and nutrition. Cash transfers can be implemented in conjunction with other services involving education, health, nutrition, and social welfare. A national system of social protection should be introduced by reaching families with capacity constrains (Adato & Bassett, 2009). Disability grants are critical for the survival of many disabled people and their families and especially important to disabled women who face further disadvantages due to their family responsibilities and greater vulnerability to HIV/AIDS and other illnesses (Goldblatt, 2009).

More HIV-positive women than HIV-positive men are attending HIV/AIDS care facilities and accessing antiretroviral medications. The values associated with masculinity cause men to take more health, economic, and social risks; therefore, institutional healthcare organizations should identify ways to reduce men's reluctance to attend care facilities (Bila & Egrot, 2009). Due to structural adjustment programs and subsidy removal relative to land and labor, female-headed households hold a disadvantaged position of depending on agricultural waged labor, making it difficult to break the poverty cycle (Takane, 2009). An HIV diagnosis can influence a mother's thoughts and actions in relation to residential and emotional security, especially on behalf of her children. Although women attempt to balance child nurturing with self-care, these efforts seldom succeed, generating high costs to their well-being and relationships with their children (Bray, 2009).

In Africa, poverty and ill-health are unequally distributed by gender, race, class, and location, creating discernible incidence patterns and coping strategies related to illnesses and deaths (Goebel, Dodson, & Hill, 2010). The genetic diversity of HIV in Africa also has a great impact on diagnosis, treatment, vaccine development, and trials (Peeters, Toure-Kane, & Nkengasong, 2003). Nevertheless, many of the large differences in the spread of HIV that have been observed within sub-Saharan Africa do not reflect biologic or behavioral factors and might have occurred due to reporting bias (Boerma, Gregson, Nyamukapa, & Urassa, 2003).

The impact of economic determinants usually depends on contextual factors. Poverty may play a role in the HIV epidemic, but its overall impact is mediated by social and behavioral factors (Nattrass, 2009). For example, being a predominantly protestant southern African country increases expected HIV prevalence while being a predominantly Muslim country reduces it. Contrary to beliefs that sexual networks in sub-Saharan Africa are too weak to sustain generalized HIV epidemics, evidence shows that the structural characteristics of such networks are compatible with the distribution of HIV among lower-risk groups (see Table 1). The unequal distribution of HIV infection within these networks accentuates the importance of the internal characteristics (Helleringer & Kohler, 2007). Specific conditions also exist, such as factors associated with an increased case-fatality rate among HIV-infected miners with tuberculosis (Churchyard et al., 2000).

Children orphaned by AIDS have more psychological issues, including depression, peer problems, post-traumatic stress, and conduct problems. Food insecurity, stigma, and bullying all increase the likelihood of psychological disorders in these children (Cluver, Gardner, & Operario, 2009; Cluver & Orkin, 2009). Food security, access to social welfare grants, employment in the household, and access to school increase their psychological health (Kim & Watts, 2005). HIV/AIDS orphans usually continue schooling, but are more likely to fall below their appropriate grade. Schooling gaps decrease at higher levels of welfare (Kasirye & Hisali, 2010). Traditional family responsibilities are being inverted as elderly family members fulfill physical and psychosocial needs of children (Nyasani, Sterberg, & Smith, 2009). The vulnerability of children in this environment of food insecurity and the weakened capacity of governments to deliver basic social services are of particular concern (Drimie & Casale, 2009). Meanwhile, socio-economic and political dilemmas of the

1989 United Nations Convention on the Rights of the Child in sub-Saharan Africa (Mulinge, 2010) continue to persist.

Human rights are applicable globally and cannot be altered according to beliefs of a single country or group of countries. Socially marginalized people have fewer opportunities to demonstrate their social value, and are at a greater risk of transmission and/or re-infection, lower adherence to medication, and require more support from services or the community (Goudge, Ngoma, Manderson, & Schneider, 2009). Research by developed countries performed on developing countries can be considered exploitation. The only way to prevent this is to insist that both informed consent be obtained and that a proven beneficial service is provided to the subjects (Annas & Grodin, 1998).

AIDS-related stigma can cause delays in testing, poor treatment adherence, and increased numbers of new infections. Increased attention on human-rights in HIV/AIDS prevention might have weakened the role of public health and social fairness, which provide a more practical framework for HIV/AIDS prevention and care (de Cock, Mbori-Ngacha, & Marum, 2002). Reconsideration of partner notification policies and greater weight on the need for emphasizing treatment are needed.

As poverty reduces access to sufficient food through decreased market purchase, land inequalities, corruption, structural adjustment programs, and civil conflict, the role of the World Trade Organization Agreement on Agriculture becomes more decisive (Mkandawire & Aguda, 2009). Effects of food insecurity in poor households with HIV infection are worsened. Food deficiency and nutritional inadequacy compromise an individual's work capacity, may further diminish their resources, (Onyango, Walingo, & Othuon, 2009), and reduce their socio-economic development (Seeley, Dercon, & Barnett, 2010). Combining traditional HIV-prevention strategies with food production and nutrition-education programs more effectively reduces the transmission risk for HIV by instituting behavioral change and an improved nutritional and immune status (Himmelgreen et al., 2009). This process also increases the life expectancy of people living with HIV/AIDS (Himmelgreen et al., 2009). Water and sanitation projects can be used as an entry point to address major HIV- and poverty-related challenges and to empower communities (Table 1). In addition to creating employment, such projects will also mobilize and address other challenges, such as gender discrimination, child abuse, and crime (Manase, Nkuna, & Ngorima, 2009). For now, complexities of translating theories of community participation into practice for hard-to-reach groups challenge attempts to improve social capital and sexual health promotion (Campbell & Mzaidume, 2001).

Table 1. Improving Social and Physical Infrastructure to Control HIV Epidemic

Problems to be Addressed	Recommendation	Strategies for Implementing Recommendations
Current program quality, coordination and resources not adequate to sustain an effective initiative over time	Adopt laws and policies to allocate sustained funding	1) Adopt national legislation that clearly empowers and funds governmental HIV control programs. 2) Promulgate, through ministry of health, education, and other relevant ministries, appropriate policies for HIV prevention. 3) Allocate funds from national budgets and from international organizations to sustain effective HIV control programs.
Lack of coordination between different sectors	Integrate service delivery	1) Coordinate central, regional, and community services. 2) Coordinate between government and nongovernment organization. 3) Develop a decentralized and integrated approach.
Mal-distribution of staff, lack of skilled staff, and training	Support human	1) Human capacity building of HIV control workers. 2) Prepare guidelines for HIV control programs and training health workers, especially nurses.
Lack of a proper surveillance and information system	Strengthen surveillance system	1) Establish and strengthen HIV sentinel surveillance. 2) Design practical systems to collect, use, and share reliable and timely data required for better programs.
Poor support from political and administrative leaders	Ensure good governance	1) Foster leadership and help modernize management. 2) Strengthen the management of procurement and logistics of HIV/AIDS related supplies
Inconsistency of financing sources	Ensure good financing	1) Strengthen performance-based financing to support the scale-up and quality improvement of programs.
Stigmatization, discrimination, and human rights abuses, lack of support from governments	Address stigma and discrimination	1) Reform policies based in deeply-rooted social attitudes and norms such as gender inequality by multi-sector collaboration. 2) Implement "know your rights campaigns" and legal support. 3) Including people living with HIV, justice systems, international organizations, and national actors in prevention programs.
Human rights of women, young people, children	Ensure human rights	1) Increase access to health education and information. 2) Ensure equal access to services by

Problems to be Addressed	Recommendation	Strategies for Implementing Recommendations
and marginalized groups are not respected		marginalized groups. 3) Ensure freedom from sexual violence, freedom from mandatory testing, the right not to be mistreated or thrown out of school on the basis of HIV status, the right to marry, and the right to work.
Lack of monitoring and evaluation	Better evaluation of program	1) Promote use of integrated indicators, resource tracking, monitoring, and evaluation of all HIV control programs. 2) Follow-up support for the family at the community level.
Lack of research on protecting women	More research	1) Understand the determinants of HIV transmission. 2) New approaches, such as microbicides, pre-exposure prophylaxis, vaccines, circumcision, female condoms, and conduct more HIV trials including women and children.
High risk behavior and high STI rates and poor discipline among military personnel both in peacetime and during conflict	Address insecurity during conflicts and emergencies	1) Prevent conditions that might force persons to sell sex to survive 2) Integrate HIV activities into disaster preparedness action plans. 3) Ensure safety during blood transfusions and surgical procedures. 4) Provide HIV prevention education to all military personnel. 5) Provide free condoms to soldiers and educate their correct use. 6) Strictly enforce military regulations related to sexual assault.
Lack of preparedness for economic downfalls	Prepare for economic crises	1) Establish an 'Early Warning System', which monitors both the current and anticipated changes in HIV/AIDS programs. 2) Improve systematic communication with stakeholders.

HIV/AIDS is the major threat to development, economic growth, and poverty alleviation in Africa. Mechanisms of the poverty/HIV/AIDS cycle should be explored (poverty increases the spread of HIV, while AIDS increases poverty, and so on), and strategies to break this cycle should be investigated. Looking beyond monetary poverty toward an understanding of these relationships is suggested (Whiteside, 2002). Effects of the HIV/AIDS epidemic in Africa have led many communities to rethink traditional customs, some responsible for exacerbating the disease's spread, some decreasing it. Recently it was found that many African students recognize the problems with gender inequities, poverty, and the adverse effects of practices perceived as western (Norton & Mutonyi, 2010).

PREVENTION

The inadequacy of current HIV prevention efforts is illustrated by the more than 2.4 million deaths and 3.2 million new HIV infections in sub-Saharan Africa in 2005 alone. Despite improvement of antiretroviral therapy (ART) programs in Africa, primary prevention efforts have not substantially improved. Cost-effectiveness summary data indicate that prevention is at least 28 times more cost effective than ART in Africa. Although funds should be allocated to ART, doing so should be in conjunction with broad population coverage by prevention programs (Marseille, Hofmann, & Kahn, 2002). A case of HIV/AIDS can be prevented for 11 US dollars and one disability adjusted life year (DALY) is gained for one US dollar by targeted prevention of sexually transmitted diseases (see Table 2). Cost-effectiveness analyses are continuously needed to evaluate these types of prevention efforts (Creese, Floyd, Alban, & Guinness, 2002).

In third-world countries, increased investment in prevention is cost-effective. Preventive strategies for persons with HIV, so-called positive prevention, help decrease their risk of infecting others. Persons living with HIV/AIDS must be active leaders in these positive prevention interventions with their dedication to the assurance "HIV stops with me." Provision of voluntary counseling and testing (VCT) to sero-discordant couples has reduced transmission significantly in Africa. Therefore, sero-status-based approaches have now become a priority in Africa and in other high-prevalence regions (de Cock, Marum, & Mbori-Ngacha, 2003). When the accessibility, affordability, and implementation potential using existing health care infrastructure are considered, additional recognized prevention strategies should include: (1) provision of HIV counseling and testing; (2) condoms to family members of persons with HIV; (3) cotrimoxazole prophylaxis; (4) isoniazid prophylaxis; (5) safe drinking water; (6) insecticide-treated bed nets; and (7) micronutrients. Several additional interventions should also be further evaluated before inclusion in a standard package of care, an important step toward reducing disparities in HIV/AIDS control (Mermin et al., 2005).

Ensuring infected individuals learn their disease status by counseling and testing in clinical, mobile, community-based, and door-to-door settings is important because disclosure of HIV status to partners may facilitate effective prevention of sexual and mother-to-child transmission (MTCT) and can ensure treatment adherence (Coetzee et al., 2005). HIV testing of partners has a significant effect because HIV discordance within couples is common in Africa. Unfortunately, many HIV-positive individuals and clinicians assume that sexual partners of infected persons have already acquired HIV and see no need for partner testing. Concurrent sexual partnerships also help to explain Africa's high HIV prevalence (Halperin & Epstein, 2004). Therefore, knowledge of partners' HIV status and safer sexual activity must be combined with fidelity by individuals with HIV (Walker, Worobey, Rambaut, Holmes, & Pybus, 2003).

Provision of ART also reduces the risk of HIV transmission by reducing viral load in the infected individual. Some studies show that providing ART is associated with reduced sexual risk behavior during the first six months of therapy, emphasizing the need for integrating ART and prevention programs (Bunnell et al., 2006). Efforts to both reduce behaviors that put others at risk and increase protective behaviors, such as abstinence, reduced frequency of sex, condom use, partner reduction, sero-sorting, and having nonpenetrative sex, should be evaluated and expanded.

Correct and consistent condom use is an effective strategy to reduce the risk of sexually transmitted infections among adolescents (Peltzer & Pengpid, 2006). Adolescents who consistently used condoms had their first sexual experience at an older age, had more condom use self-efficacy, and had a positive attitude toward safe sex compared to sporadic condom users and non-users (Kabiru & Orpinas, 2009). The theories of planned behavior (TPB) and protection motivation (PMT) can be used to predict intended condom use among adolescents (see Table 2). The significance of myths about condoms should be examined thoroughly (Boer & Mashamba, 2005). Providing life skills education for adolescents through schools and mass media is another approach to improve responsible sexual behavior, and it is proven effective in countries like South Africa (Peltzer & Promtussananon, 2003).

Doctors' attitudes, uneasiness, and lack of skills in discussing sex with their patients should be addressed to minimize transmission risk and to reduce stigma (Bunnell, Mermin, & de Cock, 2006). In places, where HIV is spreading among drug-users, interventions, such as disinfecting needles and syringes, should be implemented. In generalized epidemics, election of low-risk blood donors should be based on current HIV incidence patterns.

Contributions of unsterile health care and having multiple sexual partners are both important risk factors for HIV infections in sub-Saharan Africa (Gisselquist & Potterat, 2004). More than 90% of HIV in African adults results from heterosexual transmission, but some studies suggest a lower percentage. Additionally, the importance of medical injections and blood transfusions seems to differ from one area to another (Lepage & Perre, 1988). Therefore, re-conceptualization of research for a more accurate assessment is necessary (Gisselquist & Potterat, 2003).

The highest rates of STDs are usually found in urban men and women aged 15-35 years. On the other hand, genital ulcer disease is also more prevalent in Africa (Laga, Nzila, & Goeman, 1991). Many men in urban areas have sex with a group of prostitutes who spread STDs. In other areas, the frequent change of sex partners, economic factors, low access to health services, lack of health education, poor health seeking behavior, and lack of political motivation play roles in the spread of STDs. Promoting condom use in prostitute populations following a program of HIV education is found to be effective (Ngugi et al., 1988).

Improved STI treatment has been found to reduce HIV incidence by about 40% in rural populations (Grosskurth et al., 1995). Curable STI interventions may remain cost-saving in populations with high-risk behaviors or low male circumcision rates (White et al., 2008). Clinic-based interventions focused on STI and condom promotion can also result in a major decline of HIV-1 incidence among female sex workers (Laga et al., 1994). Female condoms and other female-controlled methods are regarded as culturally appropriate in southern Africa and are very useful. Women have been apparently asking for methods to protect themselves from HIV. Political and economic concerns combined with historical patterns of gender discrimination and the neglect of female sexuality must be viewed as the main obstacles in development of methods women can control (Susser & Stein, 2000).

HIV prevention programs must address gender inequities that place young women at greater risk for HIV infection (Pettifor et al., 2005). Women working in recreational occupations, such as tourism, to improve their income are at risk of HIV due to their dependence on sexual relationships, which take place in environments where condom use is difficult. Regardless of constraints, these women typically take action to prevent HIV by negotiating for condom use or by getting around perceived risky practices or relationships, indicating that, by perceiving their own risk, these women will welcome an effective microbicide (Lees et al., 2009). Using estimated numbers of HIV-seropositive prostitutes and their sexual contacts, it is projected that a diagnosis and treatment program of conventional STDs would be effective in preventing a large number of new HIV infections per year at a cost of only 8-12 US dollars per case prevented (Moses et al., 1991).

Table 2. Improving Prevention and Related Strategies to Control HIV Epidemic in Africa

Problems to Address	Strategies for Implementing Recommendations
Pre or extramarital partners	1) Support abstinence and faithfulness programs, target most-at-risk groups, emphasize the importance of avoiding premarital and extramarital sexual relationships, and reducing the number of sexual partners.
Poor infection	1) Promote infection control practices and 100% voluntary blood donation. 2) Universal precautions: gloves, safe disposal of needles, antiretroviral prophylaxis 3) Emphasize obligation of employers to infection control and post-exposure prophylaxis. 4) Recommendations requiring donors to fund safe injection equipment along with drugs.
Lack of motivation	1) Create social networks of people living with HIV, youths, women, human rights and faith-based organizations, AIDS services, and community groups. 2) Influence government leaders, treatment activists, and the private sector in prevention.
Unplanned programs	1) Address individual risk in certain behaviors such as use of injecting drugs. 2) Minimize reasons, such as lack of information and unavailability of condoms. 3) Address environmental and social determinants that influence risk behavior. 4) Integrated communication (advertising, peer education, and community mobilization). 5) Providing information in appropriate language in comfortable settings to each group 6) Train sex workers to provide HIV prevention education and to promote condom use. 7) Segment audience and tailor information and services to meet subpopulations' needs.
Low male circumcision rates and myths	1) Recommend male circumcision and consider it as part of HIV prevention package. 2) Train and certify circumcision providers and evaluate programs to ensure services. 3) Fight against myths and false sense of security that lead to high-risk behaviors. 4) Research effectiveness of circumcision in anal intercourse and ways to expand services.
Late postexp proph (PEP)	1) Make PEP a routine component of occupational safety policy and introduce PEP to rape survivors, refugees, sex workers, injecting drug-users, homosexuals, and prisoners.

Table 2. (Continued)

Problems to Address	Strategies for Implementing Recommendations
Unfocused programs	1) Analyze costs/benefits of different strategies and feasibility in addressing risk groups 2) Epidemiological surveillance for most effective use of resources for each risk group
Low male condom use & negotiate on power in women	1) Ensure that male condoms are consistently available and affordable to needed groups 2) Ensure leadership from all levels of society, address myths and promote gender equity. 3) Enhance knowledge on how HIV is transmitted and how condom use can reduce risk. 4) Introduce vaccines, microbicides, and female condoms to women, who face obstacles when trying to negotiate the use of male condoms.
Difficulties in reaching school children and out-of-school children and youth	1) Ensure young people's access to school or other educational HIV prevention programs. 2) Maintain high school attendance to have effective school-based sexuality education. 3) Overcome beliefs of parents that sex education encourages early sexual activity. 4) Provide life skills such as decision-making, communication and negotiation skills. 5) Use of role-plays to educate peers, where youths are trained to communicate messages. 6) Address families that cannot send children to school and children living on the streets. 7) Peer education technique, which involves out-of-school youth to convey information. 8) Street dramas to draw attention and as an alternative leisure activity to risky hobbies.
Reuse and sharing of needles and lack of IV drug-use prevention	1) Distribute disposable needles among IV drug users and instruct on proper use/disposal. 2) Conduct outreach campaigns with multisectoral collaboration for IV drug using populations regarding risk of HIV infection and importance of HIV testing. 3) Provide medical treatment for IV drug users designed to halt use of injected drugs. 4) Conduct research to determine motivations and circumstances for initiating IV drug-use and use results to design prevention interventions as appropriate.

Suggesting an explosive future HIV epidemic, young African women of 15-19 years are infected with HIV in large numbers compared to males of the same age. This fact alone has dire policy implications that demand new approaches to prevention (Laga et al., 2001). A life course approach provided within the health sector as well as in other settings and customized for different age groups should be considered for delivery of HIV prevention programming (Loewenson, Hadingham, & Whiteside, 2009).

Prevention of HIV infection in women and prevention of unintended pregnancy among infected women are the most cost-effective ways to avert HIV infection in infants. Nevertheless, mother-to-child transmission (MTCT) remains a major cause of infant morbidity and mortality in resource-poor settings. For pregnant women, only routine universal HIV testing can ensure equitable delivery of MTCT prevention (Coetzee et al., 2005). Because HIV-infected pregnant women experience great psychological distress, healthcare providers must use an approach that is more gracious as compared to existing interventions (Msellati, 2009).

Despite technical means and political will, the percentage of pregnant women involved in preventing mother-to-child transmission (PMTCT) interventions is not increasing as fast as authorities would expect. Consensus that an appropriate antiretroviral prophylactic regimen should be given to those who do not yet need ongoing therapy has been reached. Perinatal transmission of HIV type 1 contributes significantly to infant mortality, and exposure in the birth canal may account for some transmission. Manual cleansing of the birth canal with a cotton pad soaked in a microbicide has no significant impact on HIV transmission rates according to recent research, and additional methods to reduce the risk of HIV transmission during birth should be tested (Biggar et al., 1996). However, nearly half of perinatal HIV infection proved preventable with Nevirapine, which is a non-nucleoside reverse transcriptase inhibitor (NNRTI), is useful in resource-limited settings. Patient attrition and non-adherence also represent a major source of program inefficiency and should be systematically addressed (Stringer et al., 2003). Short-term (4 week) and long-term (12 month) effectiveness of a two-tiered strategy to prevent MTCT is also evident in resource-constrained settings (Tonwe-Gold et al., 2007). Infant feeding remains a major source of infection and new antiretroviral strategies are emerging with the potential to control this (Mnyani & McIntyre, 2009). Analyzing the success and failure of MTCT programs seems appropriate. A system of indicators for monitoring and evaluating programs to prevent MTCT are established, including the observation of health facilities and parental participation (Reithinger et al., 2007).

Male circumcision programs, if large scale, were found to produce major drops in HIV prevalence within a period of 10-12 years (Williams et al., 2006). Male circumcision is practiced as part of a religious ritual, as a medical treatment, or as a custom performed at initiation of adulthood. Circumcision has significantly reduced risk of HIV infection among African men, especially those who are at high risk of acquiring HIV. Acceptability and feasibility of providing large scale, but safe, services of male circumcision should be considered as an additional HIV prevention strategy where men are not traditionally circumcised (Weiss, Quigley, & Hayes, 2000). With further research to assess the feasibility, desirability, and cost-effectiveness of implementing the procedure within local contexts, inclusion of male circumcision into current HIV prevention measures is warranted (Siegfried et al., 2009). Circumcision programs for HIV negative men combined with microbicides for women appear promising (Bunnell et al., 2006).

Some research has indicated that the risk of multiple sexual partners increases with being single, being in a profession other than agriculture, being a housewife or a student, being unemployed, living in an urban area, having been raped as part of a first sexual encounter, and combining sex with alcohol. These findings can be used to develop HIV/AIDS prevention and control programs and to improve mathematical models of the epidemic (Somsé, Chapko, & Hawkins, 1993). HIV infection and intimate-partner violence share a common risk environment. A combined microfinance and training intervention can lead to reductions in intimate-partner violence in program participants. Social and economic development also have the potential to assist with these programs (Pronyk et al., 2006).

Education has been declared an effective preventative approach and the single most powerful strategy against HIV transmission. However, research on the type of education required is lacking concerning the appropriate teaching or learning methods and how such education alters student attitudes and behaviors in general. Many students criticize the excessive use of the lecture method in teaching and recommend that more visual materials, presentations by HIV-positive people and workers, and visits to relevant places should be encouraged to make a course more interesting. The significance of engaging all the pertinent stakeholders, especially the students, is stressed in developing the content of such programs (Sukati, Vilakati, & Esampally, 2010). Common characteristics of effective, engaging HIV prevention education from other countries should be considered (Herbert & Lohrmann, Submitted; Kirby, 2007; Kirby, Rolleri, & Wilson, 2007).

Conclusion

Poverty, food insecurity, lower level of education, social injustice, and violence play major roles in the African HIV epidemic worsening. This review confirms that knowledge levels about the causes and spread of STIs vary widely. Some people were well informed about issues related to protection against STIs and seeking treatment and others not at all. However, even in situations where knowledge levels are high, significant deviation in behaviors was reported. This discrepancy between awareness and behavior calls for a reorientation of sexuality education to include those elements critical for behavioral change, such as addressing gender discrepancies and, through planned intervention programs, promoting skills such as: (1) communicating effectively, (2) refusing to engage in risky behaviors, (3) negotiating use of protection, (4) correctly and consistently using condoms, and (5) seeking medical help.

This study's results also emphasize the need to re-orientate education to include the social, interpersonal, and theoretical aspects associated with difficult behavioral choices and behavioral change. This focus will reflect an understanding of the contributive factors to young people's behavioral choices, including social norms, as well as educational content that addresses the diverse needs of a wide age group that varies culturally, making the intervention context specific. A number of interventions should be designed to address the issues related to prevention skills, counseling and testing, and infrastructure development, which are briefly outlined in tables 1 and 2.

References

Adato, M., & Bassett, L. (2009). Social protection to support vulnerable children and families: the potential of cash transfers to protect education, health, and nutrition. *Aids Care-Psychological and Socio-Medical Aspects of Aids/Hiv*, *21*, 60-75.

Annas, G. J., & Grodin, M. A. (1998). Human rights and maternal-fetal HIV transmission prevention trials in Africa. *Am J Public Health*, *88*(4), 560-563.

Biggar, R. J., Goedert, J. J., Miotti, P. G., Taha, T. E., Mtimavalye, L., Justesen, A., & Waters, D. (1996). Perinatal intervention trial in Africa:

effect of a birth canal cleansing intervention to prevent HIV transmission. *The Lancet, 347*(9016), 1647-1650.

Bila, B., & Egrot, M. (2009). Gender asymmetry in healthcare-facility attendance of people living with HIV/AIDS in Burkina Faso. *Social Science & Medicine, 69*(6), 854-861.

Boer, H., & Mashamba, M. T. (2005). Psychosocial correlates of HIV protection motivation among black adolescents in Venda, South Africa. *Aids Education and Prevention, 17*(6), 590-602.

Boerma, J. T., Gregson, S., Nyamukapa, C., & Urassa, M. (2003). Understanding the uneven spread of HIV within Africa: Comparative study of biologic, behavioral, and contextual factors in rural populations in Tanzania and Zimbabwe. *Sexually Transmitted Diseases, 30*(10), 779-787.

Bray, R. (2009). How does AIDS illness affect women's residential decisions? Findings from an ethnographic study in a Cape Town township. *Ajar-African Journal of Aids Research, 8*(2), 167-179.

Bunnell, R., Ekwaru, J. P., Solberg, P., Wamai, N., Bikaako-Kajura, W., Were, W., & Mermin, J. (2006). Changes in sexual behavior and risk of HIV transmission after antiretroviral therapy and prevention interventions in rural Uganda. *Aids, 20*(1), 85-92.

Bunnell, R., Mermin, J., & de Cock, K. M. (2006). HIV prevention for a threatened continent: Implementing positive prevention in Africa. *JAMA, 296*(7), 855-858.

Campbell, C., & Mzaidume, Z. (2001). Grassroots participation, peer education, and HIV prevention by sex workers in South Africa. *Am J Public Health, 91*(12), 1978-1986.

Churchyard, G. J., Kleinschmidt, I., Corbett, E. L., Murray, J., Smit, J., & Cock, K. M. D. (2000). Factors associated with an increased case-fatality rate in HIV-infected and non-infected South African gold miners with pulmonary tuberculosis. *The International Journal of Tuberculosis and Lung Disease, 4*, 705-712.

Cluver, L., Gardner, F., & Operario, D. (2009). Poverty and psychological health among AIDS-orphaned children in Cape Town, South Africa. *Aids Care-Psychological and Socio-Medical Aspects of Aids/Hiv, 21*(6), 732-741.

Cluver, L., & Orkin, M. (2009). Cumulative risk and AIDS-orphanhood: Interactions of stigma, bullying, and poverty on child mental health in South Africa. *Social Science & Medicine, 69*(8), 1186-1193.

Coetzee, D., Hilderbrand, K., Boulle, A., Draper, B., Abdullah, F., & Goemaere, E. (2005). Effectiveness of the first district-wide programme for the prevention of mother-to-child transmission of HIV in South Africa. *Bulletin of the World Health Organization, 83*, 489-494.

Creese, A., Floyd, K., Alban, A., & Guinness, L. (2002). Cost-effectiveness of HIV/AIDS interventions in Africa: a systematic review of the evidence. *The Lancet, 359*(9318), 1635-1642.

de Cock, K. M., Marum, E., & Mbori-Ngacha, D. (2003). A serostatus-based approach to HIV/AIDS prevention and care in Africa. *The Lancet, 362*(9398), 1847-1849.

De Cock, K. M., Mbori-Ngacha, D., & Marum, E. (2002). Shadow on the continent: public health and HIV/AIDS in Africa in the 21st century. *The Lancet, 360*(9326), 67-72.

Drimie, S. & Casale, M. (2009). Multiple stressors in Southern Africa: the link between HIV/AIDS, food insecurity, poverty and children's vulnerability now and in the future. *Aids Care-Psychological and Socio-Medical Aspects of Aids/Hiv, 21*, 28-33.

Gisselquist, D. & Potterat, J.J. (2003). Heterosexual transmission of HIV in Africa: An empiric estimate. *International Journal of Std & Aids, 14*(3), 162-173.

Gisselquist, D. & Potterat, J.J. (2004). Review of evidence from risk factor analyses associating HIV infection in African adults with medical injections and multiple sexual partners. *International Journal of Std & Aids, 15*(4), 222-233.

Goebel, A., Dodson, B. & Hill, T. (2010). Urban advantage or urban penalty? A case study of female-headed households in a South African city. *Health Place, 16*(3), 573-580.

Goldblatt, B. (2009). Gender, rights, and the disability grant in South Africa. *Development Southern Africa, 26*(3), 369-382.

Goudge, J., Ngoma, B., Manderson, L., & Schneider, H. (2009). Stigma, identity and resistance among people living with HIV in South Africa. *Sahara J-Journal of Social Aspects of Hiv-Aids, 6*(3), 94-104.

Grosskurth, H., Todd, J., Mwijarubi, E., Mayaud, P., Nicoll, A., ka-Gina, G., & Mugeye, K. (1995). Impact of improved treatment of sexually transmitted diseases on HIV infection in rural Tanzania: Randomised controlled trial. *The Lancet, 346*(8974), 530-536.

Halperin, D.T. & Epstein, H. (2004). Concurrent sexual partnerships help to explain Africa's high HIV prevalence: Implications for prevention. *The Lancet, 364*(9428), 4-6.

Helleringer, S. & Kohler, H.-P. (2007). Sexual network structure and the spread of HIV in Africa: Evidence from Likoma Island, Malawi. *Aids, 21*(17), 2323-2332.

Herbert, P. & Lohrmann, D.K. (Submitted). It's all in the delivery: An analysis of instructional strategies from effective health education curricula. *Journal of School Health.*

Himmelgreen, D.A., Romero-Daza, N., Turkon, D., Watson, S., Okello-Uma, I., & Sellen, D. (2009). Addressing the HIV/AIDS-food insecurity syndemic in sub-Saharan Africa. *Ajar-African Journal of Aids Research, 8*(4), 401-412.

Kabiru, C.W. & Orpinas, P. (2009). Correlates of condom use among male high school students in Nairobi, Kenya. *Journal of School Health, 79*(9), 425-432.

Kasirye, I. & Hisali, E. (2010). The socioeconomic impact of HIV/AIDS on education outcomes in Uganda: School enrolment and the schooling gap in 2002/2003. *International Journal of Educational Development, 30*(1), 12-22.

Kim, J.C. & Watts, C.H. (2005). Gaining a foothold: Tackling poverty, gender inequality, and HIV in Africa. *BMJ, 331*(7519), 769-772.

Kirby, D. (2007). Emerging answers 2007: Research findings on programs to reduce teen pregnancy and sexually transmitted diseases. Washington, DC: The National Campaign to Prevent Teen Pregnancy.

Kirby, D., Rolleri, L., & Wilson, M. (2007). *Tool to assess the characteristics of effective sex and STD/HIV education programs.* Washington, DC: Healthy Teen Network.

Laga, M., Alary, M., Behets, F., Goeman, J., Piot, P., Nzila, N., & St Louis, M. (1994). Condom promotion, sexually transmitted diseases treatment, and declining incidence of HIV-1 infection in female Zairian sex workers. *The Lancet, 344*(8917), 246-248.

Laga, M., Nzila, N., & Goeman, J. (1991). The interrelationship of sexually-transmitted diseases and HIV-infecton: Implications for the control of both epidemics in Africa. *Aids, 5,* S55-S63.

Laga, M., Schwärtlander, B., Pisani, E., Sow, P. S., & Caraël, M. (2001). To stem HIV in Africa, prevent transmission to young women. *Aids, 15*(7), 931-934.

Lees, S., Desmond, N., Allen, C., Bugeke, G., Vallely, A., Ross, D., & Microbicides Dev, P. (2009). Sexual risk behaviour for women working in recreational venues in Mwanza, Tanzania: considerations for the acceptability and use of vaginal microbicide gels. *Culture Health & Sexuality, 11*(6), 581-595.

Lepage, P. & Perre, P.V.D. (1988). Nosocomial transmission of HIV in Africa: What tribute is paid to contaminated blood transfusions and medical injections? *Infection Control and Hospital Epidemiology, 9*(5), 200-203.

Loewenson, R., Hadingham, J., & Whiteside, A. (2009). Household impacts of AIDS: Using a life course approach to identify effective, poverty-reducing interventions for prevention, treatment and care. *Aids Care-Psychological and Socio-Medical Aspects of Aids/Hiv, 21*(8), 1032-1041.

Manase, G., Nkuna, Z., & Ngorima, E. (2009). Using water and sanitation as an entry point to fight poverty and respond to HIV/AIDS: The case of Isulabasha Small Medium Enterprise. *Physics and Chemistry of the Earth, 34*(13-16), 866-873.

Marseille, E., Hofmann, P.B., & Kahn, J.G. (2002). HIV prevention before HAART in sub-Saharan Africa. *The Lancet, 359*(9320), 1851-1856.

Masanjala, W. (2007). The poverty-HIV/AIDS nexus in Africa: A livelihood approach. *Social Science & Medicine, 64*(5), 1032-1041.

Mermin, J., Bunnell, R., Lule, J., Opio, A., Gibbons, A., Dybul, M., & Kaplan, J. (2005). Developing an evidence-based, preventive care package for persons with HIV in Africa. *Tropical Medicine & International Health, 10*(10), 961-970.

Mkandawire, P. & Aguda, N.D. (2009). Characteristics and determinants of food insecurity in sub-Saharan Africa. *Environment and Health in Sub-Saharan Africa: Managing an Emerging Crisis*, 3-23.

Mnyani, C.N. & McIntyre, J.A. (2009). Preventing mother-to-child transmission of HIV. *Bjog-an International Journal of Obstetrics and Gynaecology, 116*, 71-76.

Moses, S., Plummer, F.A., Ngugi, E.N., Nagelkerke, N.J.D., Anzalat, A.O., & Ndinya-Achola, J.O. (1991). Controlling HIV in Africa: Effectiveness and cost of an intervention in a high-frequency STD transmitter core group. *Aids, 5*(4), 407-412.

Msellati, P. (2009). Improving mothers' access to PMTCT programs in West Africa: A public health perspective. *Social Science & Medicine, 69*(6), 807-812.

Mulinge, M.M. (2010). Persistent socioeconomic and political dilemmas to the implementation of the 1989 United Nations' Convention on the Rights of the Child in sub-Saharan Africa. *Child Abuse & Neglect, 34*(1), 10-17.

Nattrass, N. (2009). Poverty, Sex and HIV. *Aids and Behavior, 13*(5), 833-840.

Ngugi, E.N., Simonsen, J.N., Bosire, M., Ronald, A.R., Plummer, F.A., Cameron, D.W., & Ndinya-Achola, J.O. (1988). Prevention of transmission of human immunodefficiency virus in Africa: Effectiveness of condom promotion and health education among prostitutes. *The Lancet, 332*(8616), 887-890.

Norton, B. & Mutonyi, H. (2010). Languaging for life: African youth talk back to HIV/AIDS research. *Language Policy, 9*(1), 45-63.

Nyasani, E., Sterberg, E., & Smith, H. (2009). Fostering children affected by AIDS in Richards Bay, South Africa: A qualitative study of grandparents' experiences. *Ajar-African Journal of Aids Research, 8*(2), 181-192.

Onyango, A.C., Walingo, M.K., & Othuon, L. (2009). Food consumption patterns, diversity of food nutrients, and mean nutrient intake in relation to HIV/AIDS status in Kisumu district Kenya. *Ajar-African Journal of Aids Research, 8*(3), 359-366.

Peeters, M., Toure-Kane, C., & Nkengasong, J.N. (2003). Genetic diversity of HIV in Africa: impact on diagnosis, treatment, vaccine development and trials. *Aids, 17*(18), 2547-2560.

Peltzer, K. & Pengpid, S. (2006). Sexuality of 16- to 17- year-old South Africans in the context of HIV/AIDS. *Social Behavior and Personality, 34*(3), 239-256.

Peltzer, K. & Promtussananon, S. (2003). Evaluation of soul city school and mass media life skills education among junior secondary school learners In South Africa. *Social Behavior and Personality, 31*(8), 825-834.

Pettifor, A.E., Kleinschmidt, I., Levin, J., Rees, H.V., MacPhail, C., Madikizela-Hlongwa, L., & Padian, N.S. (2005). A community-based study to examine the effect of a youth HIV prevention intervention on young people aged 15-24 in South Africa: Results of the baseline survey. *Tropical Medicine & International Health, 10*(10), 971-980.

Pronyk, P.M., Hargreaves, J.R., Kim, J.C., Morison, L.A., Phetla, G., Watts, C., & Porter, J.D.H. (2006). Effect of a structural intervention for the prevention of intimate-partner violence and HIV in rural South Africa: A cluster randomised trial. *The Lancet, 368*(9551), 1973-1983.

Reithinger, R., Megazzini, K., Durako, S. J., Harris, D. R., & Vermund, S. H. (2007). Monitoring and evaluation of programmes to prevent mother to child transmission of HIV in Africa. *BMJ, 334*(7604), 1143-1146.

Seeley, J., Dercon, S., & Barnett, T. (2010). The effects of HIV/AIDS on rural communities in East Africa: a 20-year perspective. *Tropical Medicine & International Health, 15*(3), 329-335.

Siegfried, N., Muller, M., Deeks, J. J., & Volmink, J. (2009). Male circumcision for prevention of heterosexual acquisition of HIV in men. *Cochrane Database of Systematic Reviews*, 2.

Somsé, P., Chapko, M.K., & Hawkins, R.V. (1993). Multiple sexual partners: Results of a national HIV/AIDS survey in the Central African Republic. *Aids*, *7*(4), 579-584.

Stringer, E.M., Sinkala, M., Stringer, J.S.A., Mzyece, E., Makuka, I., Goldenberg, R.L., & Vermund, S.H. (2003). Prevention of mother-to-child transmission of HIV in Africa: Successes and challenges in scaling-up a nevirapine-based program in Lusaka, Zambia. *Aids*, *17*(9), 1377-1382.

Sukati, C.W.S., Vilakati, N., & Esampally, C. (2010). HIV/AIDS education: What works for Swaziland University students? *Educational Research*, *52*(1), 101-113.

Susser, I., & Stein, Z. (2000). Culture, sexuality, and women's agency in the prevention of HIV/AIDS in southern Africa. *Am J Public Health*, *90*(7), 1042-1048.

Takane, T. (2009). Disparities and diversities among female-headed households in rural Malawi after 20 years of economic liberalization. *Singapore Journal of Tropical Geography*, *30*(3), 358-372.

Thurlow, J., Gow, J., & George, G. (2009). HIV/AIDS, growth and poverty in KwaZulu-Natal and South Africa: an integrated survey, demographic and economy-wide analysis. *J Int AIDS Soc*, *12*(1), 18.

Tonwe-Gold, B., Ekouevi, D.K., Viho, I., Amani-Bosse, C., Toure, S., Coffie, P.A., & Dabis, F. (2007). Antiretroviral Treatment and Prevention of Peripartum and Postnatal HIV Transmission in West Africa: Evaluation of a Two-Tiered Approach. *PLoS Med*, *4*(8), e257.

Walker, P.R., Worobey, M., Rambaut, A., Holmes, E.C., & Pybus, O.G. (2003). Epidemiology: Sexual transmission of HIV in Africa. *Nature*, *422*(6933), 679-679.

In: Contemporary Issues in Public Health
Editors: S.G. Obeng, A. Youssefagha et al.

ISBN: 978-1-63117-933-4
© 2014 Nova Science Publishers, Inc.

Chapter 6

A COMPARISON OF THE EGYPTIAN PUBLIC'S RANKINGS OF KEY PUBLIC HEALTH AND ENVIRONMENTAL ISSUES BY OCCUPATION AND BY GENDER

Ahmed Youssefagha[1], Brian Chen[1], Nargis Labib[2], David Lohrmann[1], Rasha Salama[2] and Nagla ElSherbibi[2]

[1]Indiana University, US
[2]Cairo University, Egypt

ABSTRACT

This chapter examines the public opinion of Egyptians on the priorities of public health and environmental health issues. The main aim was to examine the differences in the ranked orders based on participants' occupation and gender. There were 318 participants from Al Fayuim, Egypt, and the study took place between 2009 and 2010. A weighted ranking score system and principal component analysis were used to help provide a better confirmation of the results. To help show the relevance of the study in relation to other studies, a comparison of the top ranked public health and environmental issues with those of current World Health Organization reports was made. Results showed that maternal health and drinking water were ranked as the highest level of concern. Accident prevention and ground drinking water were as the least important public health/environmental concerns. There was a significant difference between males and females in their rankings of the public and environmental health issues, with only a slight difference between the rankings of health and non-health professional groups being noticed. The study recommends that in order to make the best strategic policy and planning decisions, health practitioners and governments must survey the opinions from a larger population sample and/or a variety of groups.

INTRODUCTION

Improving public health is both a challenge and an imperative for all the nations in Africa. The sub-Saharan region represents twenty-four percent of the global burden of disease with only thirteen percent of the world's population (Cooke, 2009). Although the burden of disease is lower per capita than for the sub-Saharan region, much remains to be done to improve the public's health in Egypt and the five other countries of North Africa. Numerous studies have documented the public health problems the region faces, including HIV/AIDS, non-communicable diseases, communicable diseases, maternal and child health, and traffic safety.

The revolutions of 2011 have changed the political landscapes for public health in the countries of North Africa. Displaced populations and violence pose immediate public health problems. Yet, in the long term, the emergence of democracies offers opportunities for individual citizens to influence the government "potentially enabling the emergence of an active civil society and investment in public health capacity, ranging from enhanced surveillance to research, training and advocacy" (Koser et al., 2011, p. 1). In order to capitalize on these new opportunities and establish effective health policies across the region, public health researchers must study the views of the citizens of the region concerning public health issues; the issues of greatest importance are most likely to receive the level of public support needed to motivate governmental action for change. Therefore, this perception study of public health issues in Egypt, conducted in 2010, is especially timely and useful.

The Egyptian government's "Health for all" and "Health in all policies" agenda led to a series of household public health surveys beginning in the early 1980s by the Egyptian Minister of Health (EMOH). The 2008 Egypt Demographic and Health Survey (EDHS), the most recent study conducted with collaboration among the EMOH, El-Zanaty and Associate Inc., and the United States Agency for International Development (USAID), provides valuable background information with implications for a study of Egyptian citizens' rankings of their most pressing public health and environmental problems.

In the 2008 EDHS study, El-Zanaty & Way (2009) provided an analysis of some of the most important public health concerns facing Egypt. These included maternal health, breastfeeding, the awareness of Hepatitis C virus, nutrition, and child health. In addition, four additional critical public health issues were identified: drug abuse control (Soueif et al., 1986); immunization (Imam, 1985); personal sanitation (WHO & UNICEF, 2010); and accident prevention (WHO, 2011)(citation needed). Traffic safety, for example, is considered one of the neglected public health challenges that receive no local or international support and yet has a critical influence on productivity and mortality rates (Cooke, 2009).

The environment often has a substantial degree of connection with public health issues such as illness, human health, mobility, and mortality. Considerable research has established that an estimated 40% of deaths worldwide result from environmental factors (Friis, 2010). Industrialization and urbanization are ongoing processes among and Northern African countries; such modernization usually results in environmental deterioration and pollution. More than two decades ago, several examples of environmental health concerns, such as water supply and sanitation in Alexandria, Egypt, were identified as being in need of improvement (Hamza, 1989). In addition, the climate change due to global warming increases the environment's impact on public health (McMichael, Woodruff & Hales, 2006). Therefore, the Egyptian government has continued its efforts to manage the environmental issues since the 1990s. The recent Egyptian Governorate's strategic plan provides detailed managerial perspectives on nine environmental issues.

This study examines the public's opinions on the priorities of ten select public health and nine select environmental health issues in Egypt and attempts to explore the differences in the relative rank ordering these issues based on different employment categories—health professionals and non-health professionals and the demographic variables of sex, age, and level of education. The research questions addressed are: 1) What differences, if any, exist between the perceptions of health professionals and non-health professionals regarding the relative importance of ten critical health issues and nine environmental health issues? 2) Do differences, if any, exist regarding perceptions of the relative importance of ten critical health issues and nine health-related environmental issues based on sex, age, and educational level?

Method

In 2010, a cohort of 354 male and female adults in Egypt was recruited to participate in the surveys with regard to the relative importance of ten public health issues and nine environmental issues. This non-probability sampling method (convenience sampling) was used with the intent to collect pilot data that can be used to inform future large-scale research in Egypt and North African countries. The response rate was 96.6%; 318 valid surveys in total were used for the analysis. Data from participants who did not follow the ranking method correctly or who returned incomplete ranking information (e.g., failure to rank all issues) were deleted.

Most public health issues in the survey were selected from the listed agendas and status reports from the 2008 EDHS. In order to find other public health issues that might attract people's attention, accident prevention (WHO, 2011), drug abuse control (Soueif et al., 1986), and personal sanitation (WHO & UNICEF, 2010) were added to the public health issue survey (citation needed). For purposes of this study, child's health was separated into two distinct categories: birth to age five years and school-aged. Thus, ten critical public health issues were identified and included in survey form for ranking of relative importance by study participants.

Hamza (1989) and Chukwuma (1995) mentioned several environmental concerns, such as water supply, air pollution, industrial pollution, and waste disposal issues, one of the first issues to come to scholarly attention. Additionally, since the early 1990s the Egyptian government has reviewed its national plans consistently and agreed on specific environmental efforts through action programs, strategies, and policies, and each Egyptian state set a series of 5-year plans for maintaining environmental affairs. The nine environmental items included on the survey used in this study were selected based on the chapters from the most current Egyptian State's Plan.

The survey was administered to two different groups of subjects—health professionals (e.g., doctors, nurses, and public health workers) and non-health professionals (i.e., the general public). These two groups were asked to prioritize the provided ten public health issues and nine environmental topics, which were accompanied with simple explanations and examples of the issues. Demographic information, such as gender, age, and educational level was collected along with the survey to provide potentially useful information in analysis (see Table 1). The survey was conducted anonymously to ensure confidentiality. Elfituri et al., (2006) had conducted a similar study in Libya (in Arabic) with surveys that were similar to those described above. This provided a reliable foundation for this study in Egypt.

Table 1. Demographic Characteristics of Subjects from the Health & Non-health Professional

Characteristic	Health Professional (n=89)		Non-Health Professional (n=229)	
	Number	%	Number	%
Sex				
Male	49	55.1	117	51.1
Female	40	44.9	112	48.9
Age				
18-24	55	61.8	143	62.4
25-40	16	18.0	45	19.7
> 40	18	20.2	41	18.0
Education level				
No Degree	4	4.4	14	6.1
High School	13	14.6	77	33.6
College Degree	56	62.9	121	52.8
Post Graduate Degree	16	18.0	17	7.4

A weighted ranking score system was used to compare the distribution of the weighted ranking among the public health and environmental issues. The issue that received the highest relative ranking was assigned 10 points (public health) or 9 points (environmental) respectively for the corresponding ranking score. The lowest ranked issue was assigned one point. The summation of multiplication of each frequency of a particular ranking by its corresponding points represents rectangular numerical integration for calculating the area underneath the digital curve (i.e., weighted ranking score) and implies the overall relative importance of a public health issue (e.g., Maternal Health) or an environmental issue (e.g., Drinking Water), in the survey.

The area under the digital curve represents the magnitude of an issue's importance, which allows for making comparisons. No differences were found between the relative rankings of health issues based on age or level of education; however, substantial differences were found based on sex of participants. Differences found based on sex of participants did not vary by occupation. The relative rank orderings by males who were employed in both health professions and non-health professions were consistent as were the relative rank orderings of females who were employed in both health professions and non-health professions. Principal component analysis (PCA) was also performed to explore the simplified "latent" factors for both the health and environmental issues and yielded implications for further discussion. The varimax rotation method was utilized for better interpretation results.

RESULTS

The top three priority public health issues for all participants were maternal health, drug abuse control, and healthy food and proper nutrition, while accident prevention received the lowest weighted ranking score. For environmental issues, the three most highly ranked items were drinking water, air and noise pollution, and human sewage. The item of least concern for all participants was ground drinking water in the environmental category (see Table 2).

Table 2. Comparison of Priority of Public Health and Environmental Issues Indicated by All Survey Participants

All participants (n = 318)			All participants (n = 318)		
Priority	Public health issue	Weighted ranking score	Priority	Environmental issue	Weighted ranking score
1	Maternal health	1931	1	Drinking water	2290
2	Drug abuse control	1854	2	Air & noise pollution	2136
3	Healthy food & proper nutrition	1805	3	Human sewage	2108
4	Child health during school age	1781	4	Household hard waste	1981
5	Child health (< 5-years-old)	1752	5	Industrial sewage/waste	1768
6	Personal sanitation	1751	6	Agricultural waste	1752
7	Immunization	1701	7	Hospital/Medical waste	1742
8	Hepatitis C virus control	1690	8	Agricultural sewage	1710
9	Breastfeeding	1652	9	Ground drinking water	1410
10	Accident prevention	1619			

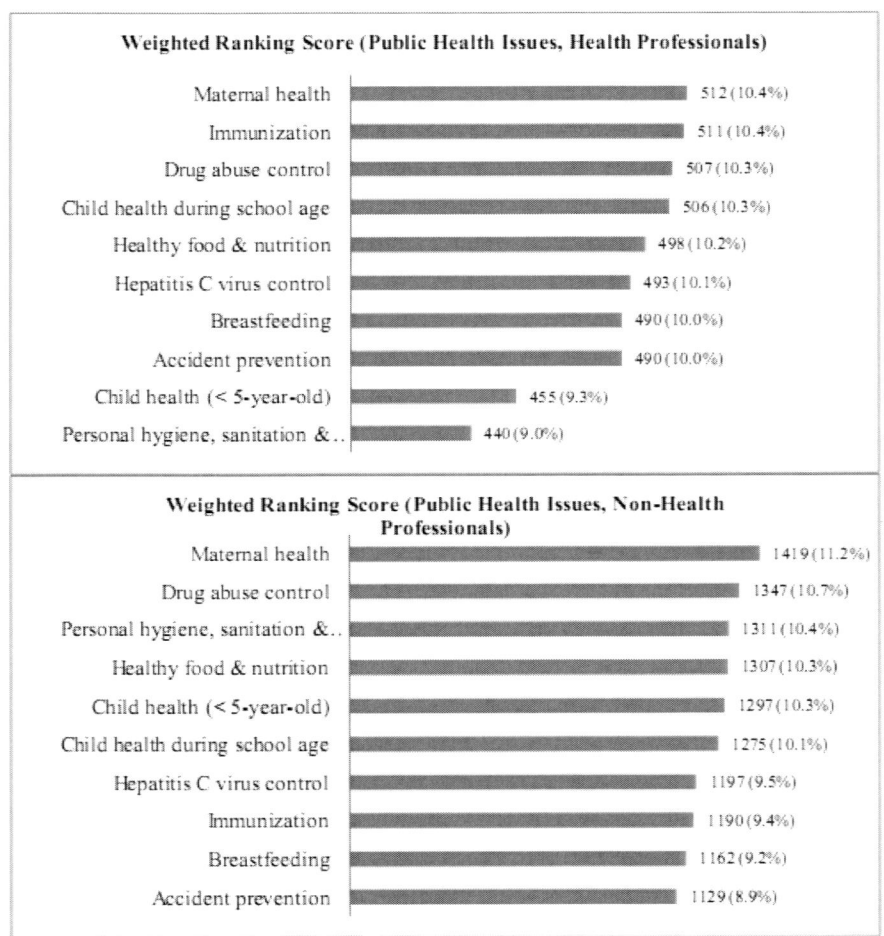

Figure 1A. Comparison of Priority of Public Health Issues Indicated by the Health Professional (n=89) & Non-health Professional (n=229) Group.

The three top priority public health issues for health professionals were maternal health, immunization, and drug abuse control. Personal sanitation received the lowest score (see Figure 1). The most important public health issue among non-health professionals was maternal health as well. Drug abuse control moved up one position to second place. While personal sanitation was at the bottom of the ranking for public health professionals, this issue had the third highest-ranking score for non-health professionals. Healthy food and nutrition was ranked fifth for public health professionals and fourth for non-health professionals. The least critical issue for non-health professional was accident prevention.

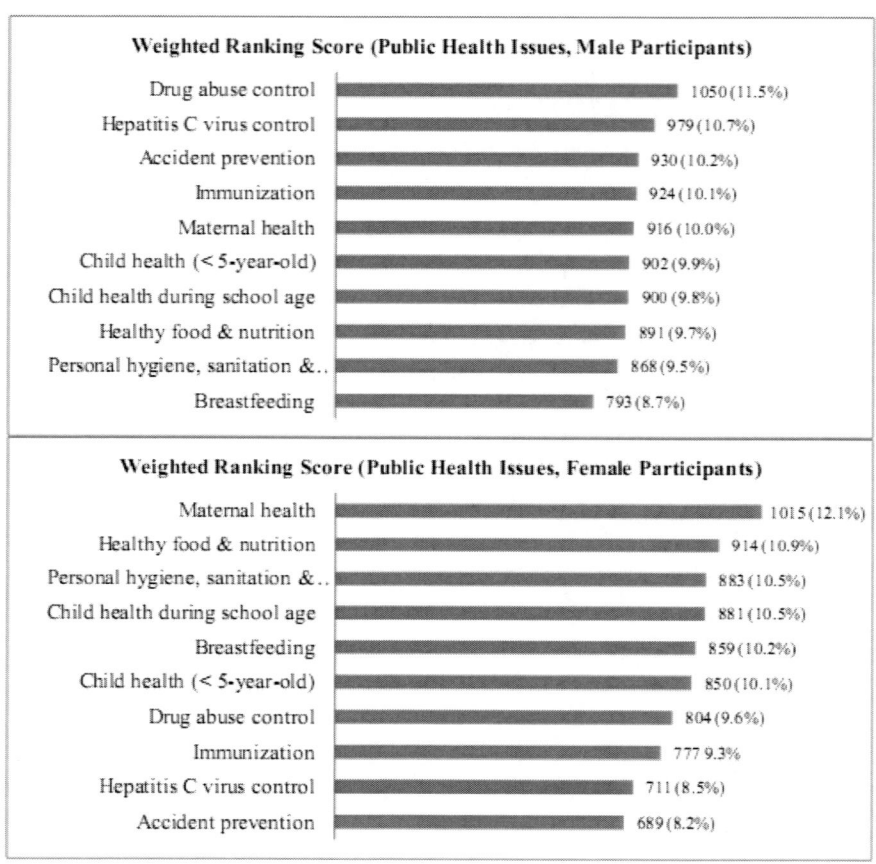

Figure 1B. Comparison of Priority of Public Health Issues Indicated by the Male (n=166) & Female (n=152) Participants.

Regarding environmental health, drinking water remained the top issue for health professionals, but dropped to second place for the non-health professional group. Essentially, the top three environmental issues were the same for all participants despite the minor differences among the weighted ranking scores. Ground drinking water was on the bottom of the priority of both health and non-health professional groups. In contrast to the health issue findings, the top three environmental issues, ranking drinking water, air, & noise pollution, and human sewage, were consistently among the top three for all participants and both the health and non-health professional groups with no differences based on age, sex, or level of education.

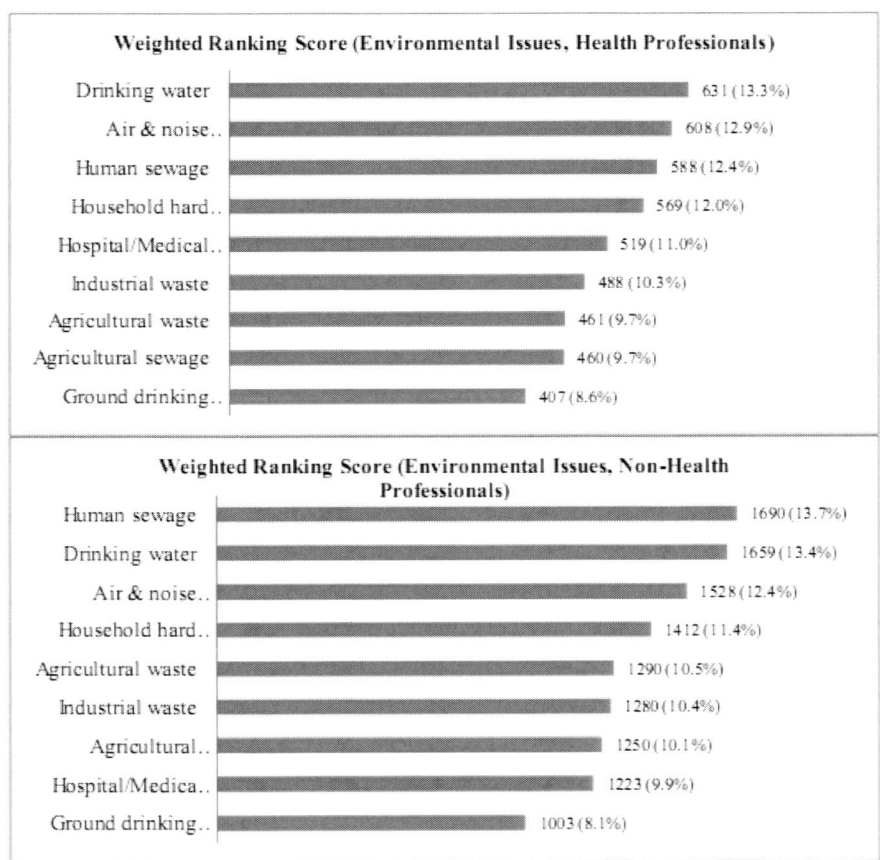

Figure 2A. Comparison of Priority of Environmental Issues Indicated by the Health Professional (n=89) & Non-health Professional (n=229) Group.

The results from PCA showed that four factors were extracted and explained 66.9% of the variations among the ten public health variables. The strategy to include a variable in a particular factor was to identify if (1) the variable had the highest loading on that factor compared to any other factor, and (2) the loading of the variable was greater than 0.45 (Cooley & Cohen, 1971; Tabachnick & Fidell, 2007). The first factor, accounting for 25.4% of the variance; the first factor includes maternal health; so it was labeled maternal health and health education. The second factor was named disease control (18.7% variance) and the third factor was referred to as nutrition and environment (12.9% variance). The fourth factor was immunization (10.0% variance) since the issue stood alone as a factor. The PCA for environmental issues produced five factors that accounted for 74% of the variance in the participants' responses; the first factor includes the issue of drinking water.

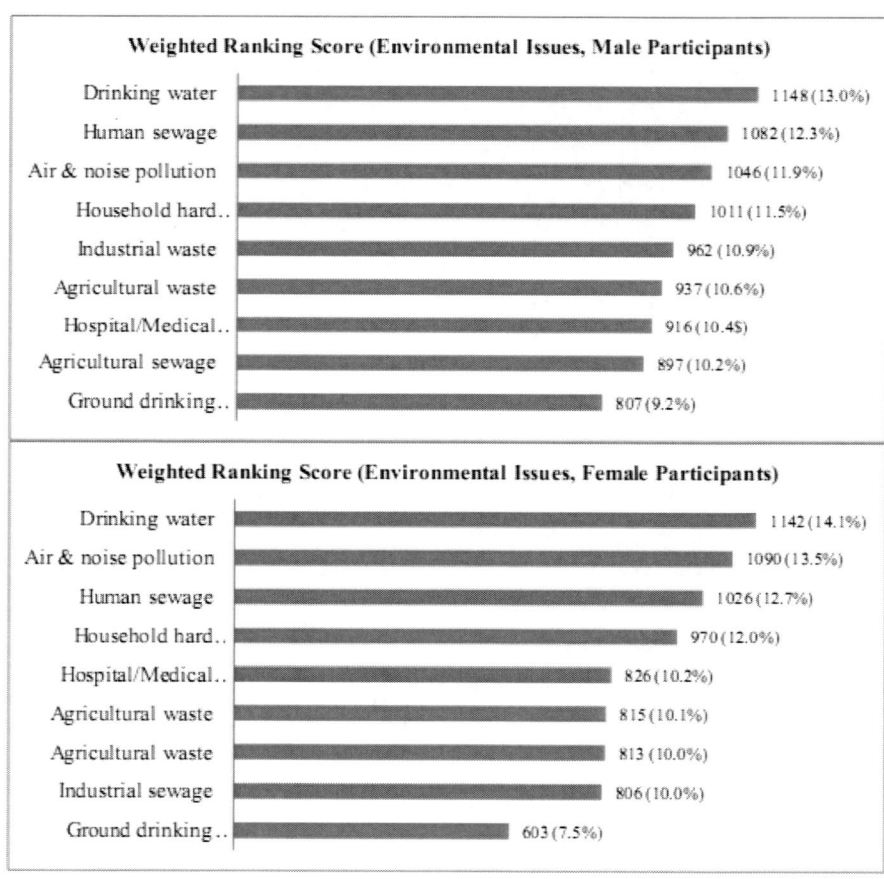

Figure 2B. Comparison of Priority of Environmental Issues Indicated by the Male (n=166) & Female (n=152) Participants.

DISCUSSION

Few studies have examined the relative level of importance of the critical public health issues in Egypt as ascribed by citizens. In general, we found that maternal health and drinking water drew the highest level of concern respectively among public health and environmental issues. Additionally, participants ranked accident prevention and ground drinking water as the least important issues respectively. Priorities were slightly different between the health and non-health professional groups for both public health and environmental issues. While men and women had similar rankings for the environmental issues, larger difference emerged between men and women in their rankings of the public health issues. Consideration of the possible reasons for these similarities and differences seems in order.

Based on weighted ranking values (the higher the value, the more critical public health issues among the subjects), the most important public health issue among all participants was maternal health. Roudi-Fahimi (2003) stated that North African and Middle East regions continue to strive for improvement of women's reproductive health, including "the poor quality of health services, widespread ignorance about reproductive health issues, financial constraints due to priorities, and continuing gender inequality. (p. 1)." Also, the extension of adolescence today may increase the chance for young people to have sexual relationships before marriage, which is a risk factor for unintended pregnancies and sexually transmitted diseases (DeJong, Shepard, Roudi-Fahimi, & Ashford, 2007). Maternal health gained first place no matter whether the subjects were health or non-health professionals (see Figure 1A). These results indicate that, in aggregate, the majority of Egyptians are well aware of the need for improvement in maternal health.

The second and third highest public health issues for health professionals were immunization and drug abuse control. One phenomenon worth noting was that personal sanitation had the lowest priority for health professionals while non-health professionals ranked this as the third most important issue. This suggests that health professionals may have a different perspective regarding the relative importance of health-related issues, perhaps because they have regular access to public health epidemiological data.

For the male and female participants, the three highest rankings differed (see Figure 1B). Perhaps the inequality of the social roles between genders (i.e., male superiority and female inferiority) led to differences in their perceptions of the relative importance of public health issues. For example, men are the dominant gender in Egyptian society, and, therefore, their rankings may indicate that women and their health during child-bearing years is of lesser importance. Or, the explanation may be as simple the differing perspectives of men and women based on the spheres of daily life they inhabit. Perhaps women cared more about domestic issues, such as, maternal health, healthy foods, and personal sanitation because these are ever-present concerns in their traditional domain. Men's traditional domain is outside the home, where accident prevention may be perceived as crucial to their health and safety. Additionally, it should be remembered that neither men nor women were necessarily saying that one issue or the other is unimportant. Rather, they were saying that, from their perspective, some issues have greater relative importance.

Maternal health was chosen from among the critical public health issue on the survey because it can be compared across the six-country North African region by using readily available WHO data. Data can be retrieved from the homepages of each profile for the examination of this public health issue (see Table 4 below).

Of the six countries, Egyptian women were ranked highest in percentage (73.6%) of those who received antenatal care by a skilled person (see Table 4, though data from Algeria and Libya were not included). Gipson et al., (2005) pointed out that Egypt was able to reduce the national maternal mortality rate (MMR) by 52% from 1992 to 2000 with donor support. A report from the collaboration of the WHO, UNICEF, UNFPA (United Nations Population Fund) and the World Bank regarding trends of worldwide maternal health in 2010, also demonstrated Egypt's improvement in maternal health with a 63% reduction in MMR between 1990 and 2008 (see Table 5 below). Even though Egypt has reduced MMR significantly, maternal health is still the top public health concern today.

In comparison, the MMR estimates for Sudan suggest that there was little, if any, sufficient progress in maternal health compared with the five other North African countries (Sudan has the lowest percent of change "-0.5"). Table 4 illustrates that 76.5% of the babies in Sudan were delivered at home while only 17.8 % of the babies were delivered in a health facility. This one figure may indicate one reason for Sudan's lack of progress in maternal health improvement.

While three of the six North African countries have recently experienced short-duration revolutions leading to changes in governments, Sudan was enveloped in armed conflict for a number of years. The lack of improved health status for women in Sudan may, at least partially, be attributable to this long-duration and wide spread civil war. It will be interesting to see if maternal health in Sudan improves now that a settlement has been achieved and if changes in maternal health status deteriorated in the three countries recently experiencing civil unrest.

Table 4. Maternal Health Data from World Health Organization (WHO)

	Egypt	Algeria	Morocco	Libya	Sudan	Tunisia
Antenatal Care (ANC)						
% of women received ANC by a skilled person	73.6	-	67.8	-	63.7	57.7
Skilled Birth Attendant (SBA) at Delivery						
% of births assisted by SBA	78.9	-	62.6	-	50.0	69.0
Place of Delivery (percentage)						
health facility	71.0	-	60.8	-	17.8	-
at home	28.2	-	38.5	-	76.5	-
other	0.8	-	0.7	-	5.7	-
Perinatal Mortality (per 1000 pregnancies)						
perinatal mortality rate (total)	19.0	-	18.6	-	-	-
perinatal mortality rate (urban)	22.0	-	15.8	-	-	-
perinatal mortality rate (rural)	17.0	-	21.3	-	-	-
neonatal mortality rate	16.0	-	27.0	-	41.0	141.0
post-neonatal mortality rate	9.0	-	14.0	-	40.0	110.0
Low Birth Weight						
% of babies weighing less than 2.5 kg	11.1	-	4.8	-	-	0.9
Fertility						
total fertility rate per woman	3.0	-	2.5	-	-	0.3
Teenage Pregnancy Rate						
% of women aged 15-19 pregnant with first child	9.6	-	2.2	-	-	1.7
Year of Survey	2008		2004		2006	1988
More Information regarding Population Structure (WHO, 2009)						
Total Population (thousands) in 2009	82999	34895	31993	6420	42272	10272
Population Living in Urban Area (%) in 2009	43	66	56	78	44	67
Birth Occurring in Urban Area (%)	62	-	50	-	-	49
Birth Occurring in Rural Area (%)	38	-	50	-	-	51

Note. Data refer to latest year available from WHO county profile database (2011). "-" represents data not available.

Table 5. Comparison of 1990, 2000, 2005, and 2008 estimates of maternal mortality ratio (MMR, deaths per 100,000 live births) in 6 North African Countries

Country	Estimated MMR[a]					% change in MMR between 1990-2008	Annual % change in MMR between 1990-2008[b]	Progress towards improving maternal health[c]
	1990	1995	2000	2005	2008			
Algeria	205	180	140	120	120	-53	-4.1	make progress
Egypt	220	150	110	90	82	-63	-5.5	on track
Libya	100	85	74	68	64	-39	-2.7	make progress
Morocco	270	220	160	130	110	-59	-5.0	make progress
Sudan	830	780	770	760	750	-9	-0.5	insufficient progress
Tunisia	130	110	83	67	60	-54	-4.3	make progress

Note. Data were retrieved from WHO, UNICEF, UNFPA, & the World Bank, 2010.
[a] The MMR have been rounded according to the following scheme: < 100, no rounding; 100-999, rounded to nearest 10; and > 1000, rounded to nearest 100.
[b] Negative values indicate a decreasing MMR from 1990 to 2008, while positive values indicate an increasing MMR. Given that the uncertainty intervals are wide for some countries, these will have to be interpreted with caution.
[c] Countries with MMR ≥ 100 in 1990 are categorized as "on track" if there has been 5.5% decline or more annually, "making progress" if MMR has declined between 2% and 5.5%, making "insufficient progress" if MMR has declined less than 2% annually, and having "no progress" if there has been an annual increase in MMR. Countries with MMR < 100 in 1990 are not categorized.

Table 6. Progress on Drinking-Water: 6 North African Country Estimates for 1990, 2000 and 2008

Country, area or territory	Year	Population (thousand)	Percentage urban population	Urban Improved Total improved	Urban Improved Piped on premises	Urban Other improved	Urban unimproved	Rural Improved Total improved	Rural Improved Piped on premises	Rural Other improved	Rural unimproved	Total Improved Total improved	Total Improved Piped on premises	Total Other improved	Total unimproved	Number of people who gained access to improved sources of drinking-water 1990-2008 (thousand)
Algeria	1990	25283	52	100	87	13	0	88	48	40	12	94	68	26	6	
	2000	30506	60	93	84	9	7	84	52	32	16	89	71	18	11	
	2008	34373	65	85	80	5	15	79	56	23	21	83	72	11	17	4764
Egypt	1990	57785	43	96	90	6	4	86	39	47	14	90	61	29	10	
	2000	70174	43	99	95	4	1	93	65	28	7	96	78	18	4	
	2008	81527	43	100	99	1	0	98	87	11	2	99	92	7	1	28706
Libya	1990	4365	76	54	-	-	46	55	-	-	45	54	-	-	46	
	2000	5346	76	54	-	-	46	55	-	-	45	54	-	-	46	
	2008	6294	78	-	-	-	-	-	-	-	-	-	-	-	-	-
Morocco	1990	24808	48	94	74	20	6	55	5	50	45	74	38	35	26	
	2000	28827	53	96	82	14	4	58	13	45	42	78	50	28	22	
	2008	31606	56	98	88	10	2	60	19	41	40	81	58	23	19	7243
Sudan	1990	27091	27	85	76	9	15	58	19	39	42	65	34	31	35	
	2000	34904	36	73	60	13	27	55	16	39	45	61	32	29	39	
	2008	41348	43	64	47	17	36	52	14	38	48	57	28	29	43	5959
Tunisia	1990	8215	58	95	89	6	5	66	22	40	38	81	61	20	19	
	2000	9452	63	98	92	6	2	77	33	44	23	90	70	20	10	
	2008	10169	67	99	94	5	1	84	39	45	16	94	76	18	6	2905

Note. Data were retrieved from WHO & UNICEF, 2010. "-" represents data not available. The less % (under the unimproved column), the better situation.

For the environmental issues, survey results indicated that the three top concerns for all groups involved in this study were drinking water, air and noise pollution, and human sewage. This indicates that participants seemed to have common perceptions regarding the most important three environmental issues. Consistently, ground drinking water was the issue that participants gave the lowest relative ranking regardless of group membership or demographic association.

In addition, the PCA results for environmental issues did not prove to be an efficient and meaningful mechanism for further grouping issues into simplified factors. However, drinking water was found to belong to the first extracted factor that had the highest percentage (19.23%) of the total variance among all variables, indicating the high relative importance of this issue. The overall results along with the PCA findings led to selection of drinking water as the environmental health issue to explore across the six North Africa nations.

Drinking water is a challenging environmental agenda for the North African countries (WHO, World Bank, UNICEF & UNFPA, 2010). Ouda et al., (2011) studied the Middle East and North Africa (MENA) region for agricultural water requirements in 2025 and concluded that a significant increase in necessary water requirements (e.g., Egypt 33%, Kuwait 29%, and Algeria 15%) will occur. From the health perspective, unsanitary and poor water quality can lead to serious gastrointestinal and infectious diseases (e.g., diarrhea, malaria, and Dengue fever) that contribute to the burden of morbidity and mortality. Moreover, water pollution from various sources, such as, air pollution and agricultural emissions, are additional risk factors that negatively influence human health (Jury & Vaux Jr., 2007). In 2007, protests occurred in Egypt with the intent of drawing Egyptian leaders' attention to the shortage of clean water. Given these facts and Egypt's geographic disadvantages (i.e., huge percentage of deserts nationwide), it was reasonable for survey respondents to choose drinking water as the top environmental issue.

Table 6 above summarizes the percentage estimates for the use of drinking water sources relative to population. Egypt had the lowest percentage of unimproved water sources (1%) while Sudan had the largest percentage (43%) of poor resources in 2008. From 1990 to 2008, Egypt, Morocco, and Tunisia made progress toward decreasing the percentage of unreliable water sources, whereas, for Algeria and Sudan access to improved drinking water sources actually declined. Libya did not have completed estimates in some of the areas, with none for the year 2008.

LIMITATIONS

One limitation of this study was the non-probability sampling method, which inhibits generalization of findings to populations beyond the participants. Larger surveys with randomized sampling would be helpful and can be conducted based on this pilot study. Such studies could include participants with a wider array of educational, and, by inference, income levels (i.e., individuals with no schooling and elementary schooling only plus more individuals high school completion). One geographical limitation is that this study does not include subjects in Egypt's Sahara region, thus, perhaps explaining the low relative importance ascribed to ground drinking water as an environmental issue. Finally, study results reflect relative perceptions of the importance of a recognized critical health or environmental issue as compared to other critical health and environmental issues. The findings do not reveal the magnitude of relative importance (i.e., issues could have been tightly clustered, evenly spaced, or widely disbursed) nor do they indicate that any of the issues were perceived to be unimportant.

This study revealed that the opinions on the ranking for public health and environmental health issues differed slightly between health and non-health professional groups. Men and women had more divergent results, especially regarding the top public health issues. Therefore, future studies should consider the confounding effect of gender. In the broadest sense, these results suggest that health practitioners and governments should survey the perceptions of various groups of people in order to better inform their strategic policy and planning decisions. Similar studies in the future conducted from a broad base of stakeholders could lead to implementation of successful and effective public health and health-related environmental interventions with wide-spread popular support. If not feasible to conduct large-scale studies, it may be sufficient to survey health professionals since their rankings differed little from those of their well-educated counterparts.

This is a key finding that could influence study design factors for MENA (e.g., cost, time, efforts). Therefore, it may be concluded that this pilot study yielded sound preliminary findings on which to base future research study directions regarding the surveyed issues. Finally, based on the cross-country comparison the results suggest that, although Egypt has improved maternal health and drinking water access compared to the other countries, these remain two of the most important concerns for Egypt's citizens.

REFERENCES

Chukwuma, C., Sr. (1995). Environmental, developmental, and health perspectives in Egypt. *Environmental Management and Health*, 6(1), 29-37.

Cooke, J.G. (2009). Public health in Africa: A report of the CSIS Global Health Policy. Washington, DC: Center for Strategic & International Studies [online]. Accessed on 2011/08/23/. Available from: http://csis.org/files/media/csis/pubs/090420_cooke_pubhealthafrica_web.pdf.

Cooley, W.W. & Lohnes, P.R. (1971). *Multivariate data analysis*. New York: Wiley.

DeJong, J., Shepard, B., Fahimi-Roudi, F., & Ashford, L. (2007). Young people's sexual and reproductive health in the Middle East and North Africa. Washington, DC: Population Reference Bureau [online]. Accessed on 2011/08/12/?]. Available from: http://www.prb.org/pdf07/MENA youthreproductivehealth.pdf.

El-Zanaty, F., & Way, A. (2009). Egypt demographic and health survey 2008. Cairo, Egypt: Ministry of Health, El-Zanaty and Associates, and Macro International [online]. Accessed on 2011/08/14.?]. Available from: http://www.measuredhs.com/pubs/pdf/FR220/FR220.pdf.

Elfituri, A.A., Elmahaishi, M.S., MacDonald, T.H. & Sherif, F.M. (2006). Health education in the Libyan Arab Jamahiriya: Assessment for future needs. *Eastern Mediterranean Health Journal*, 12(Suppl. 2), S147-155.

Gipson, R., El Mohandes, A., Campbell, O., & Issa, A.H. (2005). The trend of maternal mortality in Egypt from 1992-2000: An emphasis on regional differences. *Maternal and Child Health Journal*, 9(2), 71-82.

Hamza, A. (1989). An appraisal of environmental consequences of urban development in Alexandria, Egypt. *Environment and Urbanization*, 1(1), 22-30.

Imam, I. Z. (1985). Immunization and primary health care in Egypt. *Trop Geogr Med.*, 37(3), S65-6.

Jury, W.A., & Vaux, Jr., H.J. (2007). The emerging global water crisis: Managing scarcity and conflict between water users. *Advances in Agronomy*, 95, 1-76.

Koser, K., Mhirsi, Z., London School of Hygiene & Tropical Medicine, & European Centre on Health of Societies in Transition. (2011). The Arab Spring: a new awakening for public health? Series of Global Health Lab Discussions. London, UK; 2011/09/06.

McMichael, A.J., Woodruff, R.E., & Hales, S. (2006). Climate change and human health: Present and future risks. *The Lancet, 367*(9513), 859-869.

Nyamtema, A.S., Urassa, D.P., & Van Roosmalen, J. (2011). Maternal health interventions in resource limited countries: A systematic review of packages, impacts and factors for change. *BMC Pregnancy and Childbirth, 11*(30), 1-12.

Ouda, S., El Afandi, G., & Abd El-Hafez, S. (2011). Prediction of total water requirements for agriculture in the Arab world under climate change. Fifteenth International Water Technology Conference, IWTC-15 2011, Alexandria, Egypt.

Roudi-Fahimi, F. (2003). Women's reproductive health in the Middle East and North Africa. Washington, DC: Population Reference Bureau [online]. Accessed on 2011/09/04.?]. Available from: http://www.prb.org/pdf/WomensReproHealth_Eng.pdf.

Soueif, M. I., Yunis, F. A., Taha, H. S. (1986). Extent and patterns of drug abuse and its associated factors in Egypt. *Bull Narc.*, 38(1-2), 113-20.

Tabachnick B.G., & Fidell L.S. (2007). *Using multivariate statistics* (5th edition). Boston: Pearson.

World Health Organization. (2011). Violence and Injury Prevention: Road safety in Egypt. [online]. Accessed on 2012/07/09. Available from http://www.who.int/violence_injury_prevention/road_traffic/countrywork/egy/en/index.html

World Health Organization. (2011). Egypt country health profile, immunization and maternal health profile [online]. Accessed on 2012/08/04. Available from: http://www.who.int/countries/egy/en/

World Health Organization. (2011). Morocco country health profile, immunization and maternal health profile [online]. Accessed on 2012/08/06. [cited ???] Available from: http://www.who.int/countries/mar/en/

World Health Organization. (2011). Sudan country health profile, immunization and maternal health profile [online]. Accessed on 2012/08/07. Available from: http://www.who.int/countries/sdn/en/

World Health Organization. (2011). Tunisia country health profile, immunization and maternal health profile [online]. Accessed on 2012/08/11. Available from: http://www.who.int/countries/tun/en/

World Health Organization & United Nations Children Fund. (2010). Progress on sanitation and drinking-water [online]. Accessed on 2012/08/15. Available from: http://whqlibdoc.who.int/publications/2010/9789241563956_eng_full_text.pdf.

World Health Organization, World Bank, United Nations Children Fund & United Nations Population Fund. (2010). Trends in maternal mortality: 1900 to 2008 [online]. Accessed on 2012/08/15. Available from: http://whqlibdoc.who.int/publications/2010/9789241500265_eng.pdf.

EDITORS' CONTACT INFORMATION

Professor Samuel Gyasi Obeng
African Studies Program & School of Global and International Studies
Indiana University, Woodburn Hall 221
Bloomington IN 47405
sobeng@indiana.edu

Dr. Ahmed Youssefagha
The School of Public Health & African Studies Program
Indiana University, 1025 E. 7th Street, Suite 111
Bloomington IN 47405

Dr. Wasantha Parakrama Jayawardene, MD, MPH
The School of Public Health & African Studies Program
Indiana University, 1025 E. 7th Street, Suite 111
Bloomington IN 47405

INDEX

#

21st century, 83

A

abuse, 94, 95
access, 21, 45, 48, 70, 71, 72, 76, 78, 85, 99, 103, 104, 105
accessibility, 21, 74
accident prevention, xii, 91, 92, 94, 96, 99, 100
accounting, 97
ADA, 4, 5, 8, 23, 31
adaptation, xii, 52, 53, 65, 66
adolescents, 67, 75, 82
adulthood, 80
adults, 10, 11, 12, 13, 14, 15, 20, 32, 75, 83, 92
adverse effects, 58, 74
advocacy, 90
Afghanistan, 23, 24, 44
Africa, v, vi, ix, x, xii, 20, 35, 37, 41, 42, 47, 54, 57, 59, 60, 67, 68, 69, 70, 73, 74, 75, 76, 77, 81, 82, 83, 84, 85, 86, 87, 90, 104, 106
age, 4, 5, 6, 7, 8, 9, 14, 36, 37, 41, 43, 68, 75, 78, 81, 91, 92, 93, 94, 97
agricultural sector, 52, 64

agriculture, xi, 51, 52, 53, 54, 55, 56, 57, 58, 60, 61, 62, 63, 64, 65, 66, 80, 107
AIDS, ix, 68, 69, 70, 71, 73, 74, 77, 82, 85, 86, 87
Al Fayuim, xii, 89
Alaska, 11, 12
Alaska Natives, 11
Albania, 42
Algeria, xi, 23, 24, 33, 51, 57, 59, 61, 63, 64, 100, 101, 102, 103, 104
alters, 80
ANC, 68, 101
ANOVA, 28, 54
antibody, 45
antigen, 41, 42, 45
aquifers, 64
Arab countries, xi, 51, 52, 53, 58, 64, 65, 66
Arab world, xi, 65, 107
Arabian Peninsula, v, ix, 1
Arabic Center for Dry and Arid Zones Studies, xi, 51
armed conflict, 100
Armenia, 23, 24
Asia, 10, 54, 55, 56, 58
Asian Americans, 2
assault, 73
assessment, 48, 53, 76
assets, 25
asylum, 25, 37, 41
asymmetry, 82
asymptomatic, xi, 36, 39, 45, 46

attitudes, 75, 80
authorities, 79
awareness, xii, 14, 16, 81, 91

B

background information, 91
Bahrain, xi, 3, 23, 24, 51, 56, 58, 59, 61, 62
Baluchistan, 17, 31, 33
Bangladesh, 2, 3, 13, 16
barriers, xi, 15, 45, 46
base, 54, 105
beer, 24
behavioral change, xii, 71, 81
behavioral choices, xii, 81
behaviors, xii, 12, 75, 76, 77, 80, 81
Belgium, 34, 49
benefits, 78
beverages, 24
bias, 70
Bio-Statistics, ix
birth weight, 2
births, 101, 102
Blacks, 2
blood, 2, 21, 36, 46, 73, 75, 76, 77, 85
blood transfusion(s), 36, 73, 76, 85
blood vessels, 2
body mass index, 14
Brazil, 2, 18
breastfeeding, 91
bullying, 70, 82
Burkina Faso, 68, 82
Burma, 44
Burundi, 44, 68

C

Cairo, 106
calorie, 29
Cameroon, 14
campaigns, 72, 78
capacity building, 72
carbohydrates, 21
carcinoma, 48

cardiovascular disease, 2, 16
cardiovascular risk, 13, 33, 34
Caribbean, 54
case study, 83
cash, 81
CDC, 39, 40
centigrade, 53
Central African Republic, 87
central obesity, 6, 8
challenges, 48, 66, 68, 71, 87, 91
child abuse, 71
children, 42, 43, 70, 72, 73, 78, 81, 82, 83, 86
Chile, 16
China, 2, 12, 14, 15
cholesterol, 2, 31
chronic, xi, 2, 36, 40, 42, 43, 46, 47, 48
circumcision, 36, 37, 73, 76, 77, 79, 87
cirrhosis, 36, 40, 43
citizens, 90
citizenship, 25
City, 12, 39, 49
civil society, 90
civil war, 100
clients, 39
climate(s), 22, 51, 52, 53, 54, 55, 58, 59, 60, 61, 64, 65, 66, 91, 107
climate change, 51, 52, 53, 54, 58, 59, 60, 61, 64, 65, 66, 91, 107
collaboration, 49, 72, 78, 90, 100
Colombia, 44
communication, 73, 77, 78
community(ies), 10, 11, 12, 15, 31, 48, 71, 72, 73, 74, 77, 86
Community Health, ix
community service, 72
compliance, 15
complications, 2, 16, 33
conceptualization, 76
condoms, xii, 67, 73, 74, 75, 76, 77, 78, 81
confidentiality, 92
conflict, 71, 73, 106
Congo, 44
congress, 38, 43, 44
Consensus, 79

Index

consulting, 18
consumption, x, 3, 9, 19, 21, 24, 27, 28, 29, 31, 63, 86
consumption patterns, 21, 86
coordination, 72
coping strategies, 70
coronary artery disease, 11
correlation(s), 29, 37
corruption, 71
cost, 74, 76, 79, 80, 85, 105
Côte d'Ivoire, 68
cotton, 79
counseling, xii, 45, 74, 81
country of origin, 25, 42
crises, 73
crop(s), 21, 53, 58, 66
Cuba, 44
cultural differences, xi
culture, 5, 9, 21, 30, 44, 46
curricula, 84

D

data analysis, 30, 106
data availability, 52
data collection, 30, 31
database, 60, 65, 101
death rate, 20
deaths, 68, 70, 74, 91, 102
Decision Science, ix
deficiency(ies), 67, 71
degradation, 25
Department of Health and Human Services, 38, 43, 44
Department of Homeland Security, 38, 43, 44, 47
depreciation, 25
depression, 70
depth, ix
detection, 8, 17
developed countries, 8, 36, 71
developing countries, 21, 33, 36, 71
deviation, xii, 81
DHS, 38

diabetes, v, ix, x, 1, 2, 3, 4, 5, 6, 7, 8, 9, 10, 11, 12, 13, 14, 15, 16, 17, 18, 19, 20, 21, 22, 23, 24, 26, 27, 28, 29, 30, 31, 32, 33, 34
diabetic nephropathy, 2
diabetic neuropathy, 2
diabetic patients, 15
diabetic retinopathy, 2
diagnostic criteria, 2
diarrhea, 104
diet, x, 3, 19, 21, 22
dietary habits, 1
disability, 74, 83
disaster, 73
disclosure, 74
discordance, 75
discrimination, 67, 71, 72, 76
disease control, xiii, 98
diseases, xi, 35, 42, 46, 84, 90, 104
disposable income, 29
distribution, xii, 29, 30, 58, 70, 72, 93
diversity, 68, 86
Djibouti, xi, 38, 43, 57, 59, 60, 62, 64
doctors, 92
domestic issues, 99
domestic violence, 46
donors, 75, 77
draft, 66
drawing, 104
drinking water, xii, 74, 89, 94, 96, 98, 99, 104, 105
drug abuse, 91, 92, 94, 95, 99, 107
drug interaction, 46
drug treatment, 39, 49, 50
drugs, 46, 77, 78
dyslipidemia, 14

E

Eastern Europe, 42
ecological perspective, x
economic development, x, 19, 20, 21, 30, 52, 71, 80
economic growth, 69, 73
economic liberalization, 87

economic systems, 20
education, xii, xiii, 37, 45, 46, 67, 69, 71, 72, 73, 75, 76, 77, 78, 80, 81, 82, 84, 86, 87, 106
Egypt, xi, xii, 1, 3, 13, 23, 24, 32, 34, 36, 48, 49, 51, 53, 57, 59, 62, 63, 64, 65, 89, 90, 91, 92, 93, 98, 100, 101, 102, 103, 104, 105, 106, 107
election, 75
elementary school, 105
employers, 77
employment, 37, 70, 71, 91
energy, 64
environment(s), xiii, 70, 76, 80, 91, 98
environmental effects, 52
environmental factors, 91
environmental health, xii, 89, 91, 104, 105
environmental issues, xii, 89, 91, 92, 93, 94, 96, 98, 99, 104, 105
epidemic, ix, xii, 1, 3, 9, 13, 33, 67, 68, 69, 70, 73, 78, 80, 81
epidemiology, 16, 17, 33
equipment, 36, 46, 77
Eritrea, 38, 43, 44
ethnic groups, 2, 8, 11
ethnicity, 31
ethnographic study, 82
evaporation, 52
evapotranspiration, 53
evidence, 36, 69, 70, 83, 85
expenditures, 20
exploitation, 71
exposure, 36, 41, 42, 45, 73, 77, 79
extraction, 25
extreme weather events, 52

F

fairness, 71
faith, 77
families, 45, 69, 78, 81
family history, 6, 8, 9, 15
family members, 70, 74
fasting, 2, 3, 9, 10, 11, 12, 13, 16, 17, 31
fasting glucose, 2, 10, 11, 12, 13, 17, 31

fat, x, 3, 19, 21, 24, 27, 28, 29, 31
fear, 37, 46
feelings, 39
fertility, 101
fertility rate, 101
fever, 104
fidelity, 75
field crops, 65
financial, 99
fish, 29
floods, 52
food, x, xii, 1, 3, 9, 21, 22, 24, 28, 29, 30, 32, 52, 64, 67, 70, 71, 81, 83, 85, 86, 94, 95
food habits, 1
food production, 21, 64, 71
food security, x, 30, 64
force, 73
Ford, 12
France, 41
freedom, 72
fruits, 21
funding, 72
funds, 72, 74

G

GDP, x, 25, 29, 30
GDP per capita, 25, 30
gender differences, 68
gender discrepancies, xii, 81
gender equity, 78
gender inequality, 72, 84, 99
general practitioner, 18, 45
genetic diversity, 70
genetic predisposition, 3, 9
genetics, 11
genotype, 22, 33
Georgia, 41
global warming, 91
glucose, x, 1, 2, 10, 11, 12, 13, 14, 15, 16, 17, 18, 31, 32, 33, 34
glucose regulation, 11, 12
glucose tolerance, x, 1, 2, 11, 12, 13, 14, 15, 16, 17, 18, 31, 32

gonorrhea, 42
governance, 72
government funds, 42
governments, xii, xiii, 28, 65, 70, 72, 90, 100, 105
grants, 69, 70
Greece, 16, 41, 42
gross domestic product, 25
Gross Domestic Product, 26
ground drinking water, xii, 89, 94, 99, 104, 105
group membership, 104
grouping, 104
growth, 87
guidelines, 72
Guinea, 10

H

HAART, 85
harvesting, 65
HBV, xi, 36, 37, 38, 40, 41, 42, 43, 46
HCC, 36, 46
health, ix, xi, xii, 11, 14, 15, 16, 20, 22, 30, 32, 36, 45, 46, 48, 69, 70, 72, 74, 75, 76, 79, 81, 84, 86, 89, 90, 91, 92, 93, 94, 95, 96, 97, 99, 100, 101, 104, 105, 106, 107
health care, xi, 14, 46, 48, 74, 75, 106
health care system, 46
health education, 46, 72, 76, 84, 86, 97
health practitioners, xiii, 90, 105
health problems, 90
health researchers, 90
health services, 45, 76, 99
health status, 100
height, 14, 21
hepatitis, ix, x, 35, 36, 37, 39, 40, 41, 42, 43, 45, 46, 47, 48, 49, 50
hepatitis A, ix, 45
Hepatitis B, v, x, 35, 39, 40, 41, 42, 47, 48, 49
Hepatitis C, 36, 40, 47, 48, 49, 91, 94
hepatitis E, 41
hepatocellular carcinoma, 36
high fat, 9

high fiber foods, 21
high prevalence of diabetes, 12, 21, 22
high school, 78, 84, 105
history, 2, 8, 9, 37, 44, 45, 46
HIV, vi, ix, xii, 37, 41, 45, 46, 49, 67, 68, 69, 70, 71, 72, 73, 74, 75, 76, 77, 78, 79, 80, 81, 82, 83, 84, 85, 86, 87, 90
HIV and AIDS, ix
HIV test, 75, 78, 79
HIV/AIDS, vi, 67, 68, 69, 70, 71, 72, 73, 74, 80, 82, 83, 84, 85, 86, 87, 90
HIV-1, 76, 84
homosexuals, 77
hub, 36
human, 22, 37, 42, 66, 67, 71, 72, 77, 86, 91, 94, 96, 104, 107
human development, 66
Human Development Report, 66
human health, 91, 104, 107
human immunodeficiency virus, 37
human rights, 67, 72, 77
hypertension, 14, 16, 17, 18
hypothesis, 8, 9, 30
hypothesis test, 30

I

identification, 47
identity, 83
IGT, x, 4, 5, 6, 9, 16
immigrants, 15, 42, 45, 46, 47
Immigration and Nationality Act, 38, 43, 44
immunity, 45
immunization, xi, xiii, 35, 42, 43, 46, 49, 91, 95, 98, 99, 107
immunodeficiency, 42
imports, 52
impotence, 2
incidence, xi, 2, 21, 22, 35, 39, 42, 43, 46, 70, 75, 76, 84
income, 19, 20, 69, 76, 105
increased access, 21, 30
incubation period, 36
independent variable, 54
India, 2, 15, 16, 17

Indians, 2, 12
individuals, 2, 30, 37, 42, 45, 74, 105
Indonesia, 3, 15
inefficiency, 79
inequality, xiii, 99
infant mortality, 79
infants, 79
infection, x, 35, 36, 39, 40, 41, 42, 45, 46, 47, 67, 68, 70, 71, 76, 77, 78, 79, 80, 83, 84
inferiority, 99
informed consent, 71
infrastructure, xii, 67, 69, 74, 81
infrastructure development., xii
inhibitor, 79
initiation, 80
injections, 76, 83, 85
injury(ies), 46, 107
insecticide, 74
insecurity, xii, 67, 70, 71, 73, 81, 83, 84, 85
insulin, 2, 9, 11
integration, 93
intercourse, 77
interface, 46
International Diabetes Federation, x, 3, 13, 22, 32, 34
intervention(s), xii, 46, 67, 74, 76, 78, 79, 80, 81, 82, 83, 85, 86, 105, 107
investment, 74, 90
Iowa, 66
Iran, 23, 24, 44
Iraq, xi, 23, 24, 41, 44, 47, 55, 56, 58, 61, 62
irrigation, xi, 51, 54, 55, 58, 60, 65
isoniazid, 74
issues, ix, xii, 20, 29, 30, 70, 81, 89, 90, 91, 92, 93, 94, 95, 96, 98, 99, 104, 105
Italy, 2, 41, 49

J

Japan, 2, 17
Jordan, xi, 10, 23, 24, 55, 56, 58, 61, 62, 65
judiciary, 38, 43, 44

K

Kenya, 11, 38, 43, 68, 84, 86
kilocalories, x, 19, 27, 28
Kurds, 47
Kuwait, xi, 3, 9, 23, 31, 56, 58, 61, 62, 104

L

lack of screening, xi
landscapes, 90
language barrier, 45
Laos, 44
Latin America, 12, 54
laws, 72
lead, 2, 77, 80, 104, 105
leadership, 72, 78
learners, 86
learning, 80
Lebanon, xi, 23, 24, 33, 56, 58, 59, 61, 62, 63
legislation, 72
leisure, 21, 78
level of education, xii, 81, 91, 93, 97
Liberia, 44
Libya, xi, 13, 23, 24, 57, 59, 60, 62, 64, 92, 100, 101, 102, 103, 104
life course, 78, 85
life expectancy, 71
lifestyle changes, x, 13, 19, 20, 21
literacy, 44
literacy rates, 44
liver, 36, 40, 43, 46, 48
liver cancer, 36
liver disease, 40, 43, 46, 48
liver failure, 36
liver transplant, 36, 40
liver transplantation, 36, 40
logistics, 72
Louisiana, 12
low prevalence of diabetes, x, 19, 22

M

magnitude, 93, 105
majority, 7, 38, 41, 64, 68, 99
malaria, 104
management, 10, 14, 45, 47, 49, 52, 53, 54, 65, 72
Maraca, xi
mass, 21, 44, 75, 86
mass media, 21, 75, 86
materials, 80
maternal health, xii, 89, 91, 94, 95, 97, 99, 100, 102, 105, 107
matter, 99
Mauritania, xi, 57, 59, 61, 63
Mauritius, 3
measurement(s), 52, 54
meat, x, 19, 24, 28, 29
media, 21, 106
medical, xii, 36, 46, 47, 76, 78, 79, 81, 83, 85
medication, 71
medicine, 46, 48
Medicine, ix, 31, 32, 47, 48, 82, 85, 86, 106
Mediterranean, 32, 33, 34, 52, 55, 65, 106
Medline search, x, 4
mellitus, 10, 11, 12, 13, 14, 15, 16, 17, 18, 31, 32, 33, 34
membership, 37
MENA region, x, 19, 23, 29, 30
menopause, 14
mental disorder, 42
mental health, 82
messages, 78
metabolic changes, 31
metabolic disorder, 8, 9
metabolic syndrome, 31
metabolism, 2, 17
methodology, 24
Mexico, 3, 10
micronutrients, 74
Middle East, i, iii, v, ix, x, 19, 20, 21, 22, 30, 32, 48, 66, 99, 104, 106, 107
migration, 41
military, 73

misconceptions, 32
models, 52, 80
modernization, 91
Mongolia, 17
Montenegro, 17
morbidity, 42, 79, 104
Morocco, 23, 24, 34, 57, 59, 61, 63, 64, 101, 102, 103, 104, 107
mortality, xi, 20, 47, 48, 49, 79, 91, 100, 101, 102, 104, 106, 108
mortality rate, xi, 20, 47, 48, 91, 100, 101
Moses, 76, 85
motivation, 75, 76, 77, 82
MR, 100
multi-ethnic, 33
multiplication, 93
multivariate statistics, 107

N

National Health and Nutrition Examination Survey, 48
national income, 21
National Survey, 34
nationality, 37, 38, 47
natural resources, 25
Nauru, 3
neglect, ix, 76
negotiating, xii, 76, 81
negotiation, 78
Nepal, 17
neutral, 52
New England, 48
Nigeria, 68
Nile, 36
non-probability sampling method, xiii, 92
North Africa, i, iii, v, ix, x, xiii, 19, 22, 52, 66, 90, 92, 99, 100, 102, 103, 104, 106, 107
North America, 20
NRT, 79
nurses, 72, 92
nutrient(s), 86
nutrition, xiii, 69, 71, 81, 91, 94, 95, 98

O

obesity, 2, 6, 8, 9, 10, 12, 14, 15, 16, 17, 18, 22
obstacles, 76, 78
officials, 24
oil, 21
oil production, 21
Oman, xi, 3, 23, 24, 31, 56, 58, 59, 60, 62, 64
operations, 49
opportunities, 37, 71, 90
organs, 36
outreach, 78
overnutrition, 33
overweight, 21, 22

P

Pacific, 2, 11
Pacific Islanders, 2
Pakistan, 2, 3, 17, 23, 24, 33, 34
Palestine, xi, 55, 56, 58, 61, 62
Paraguay, 13
parasitic infection, 48
parental participation, 79
parents, 78
participants, ix, xii, 5, 7, 80, 89, 92, 93, 94, 96, 98, 99, 104, 105
pathways, 69
PCA, 93, 97, 104
PEP, 77
per capita income, 21
percentile, 23
perinatal, 79, 101
personal communication, 31
Philadelphia, 47
Philippines, 11
physical activity, 3, 9, 20, 21
physical inactivity, 10
pilot study, 105
planning decisions, xiii, 90, 105
plants, 66
policy, ix, xiii, 53, 65, 66, 77, 78, 90, 105

policy makers, 65
pollution, 91, 92, 94, 96, 104
popular support, 105
population, x, xiii, 4, 10, 11, 12, 13, 14, 15, 16, 17, 18, 19, 20, 22, 24, 25, 26, 28, 29, 30, 32, 33, 36, 38, 39, 41, 46, 52, 53, 56, 57, 63, 64, 65, 69, 74, 90, 104
population density, 64
population group, 26
population growth, 63, 65
poverty, xii, 66, 69, 70, 71, 73, 82, 83, 84, 85, 87
poverty alleviation, 73
precipitation, 52
pregnancy, 14, 79, 84
preparedness, 73
president, 38, 43, 44
prevalence rate, 29, 31
prevention, x, xii, 3, 20, 47, 67, 69, 71, 72, 73, 74, 75, 76, 77, 78, 79, 80, 81, 82, 83, 85, 86, 87, 89, 94, 107
principal component analysis, xii, 89
prisoners, 77
private sector, 77
probability, xiii, 2, 92, 105
probability sampling, xiii, 92, 105
procurement, 72
producers, 25
professionals, 91, 92, 95, 96, 99, 105
programming, 79
project, 12
proliferation, 21
prophylactic, 79
prophylaxis, 73, 74, 77
protection, xii, 37, 69, 75, 81, 82
psychological distress, 79
psychological health, 70, 82
public health, ix, xii, 42, 47, 68, 71, 83, 85, 89, 90, 91, 92, 93, 94, 95, 97, 98, 99, 100, 105, 106
Public Health, i, ii, iii, vi, ix, 13, 15, 16, 19, 48, 49, 81, 82, 87, 89, 94, 95, 96
public opinion, 89
public support, 90

Q

Qatar, xi, 11, 23, 24, 56, 58, 61, 62
quality improvement, 72
quantification, 53
questionnaire, xii

R

race, 37, 70
rainfall, 52, 64
randomized sampling, 105
rape, 77
recreational, 76, 84
reform, 72
refugee admission, 38, 43, 44
refugee status, 37
refugees, x, 25, 35, 36, 37, 38, 39, 41, 42, 44, 45, 46, 47, 48, 49, 77
regions of the world, x, 1, 9
regression, xi, 53, 54, 60, 61, 62, 65
regression analysis, 53, 65
regression equation, 54
regulations, 73
relevance, xii, 89
reliability, 42
religion, x, 3, 9, 37
requirements, xi, 38, 43, 44, 53, 54, 65, 104, 107
researchers, xii
resistance, 83
resources, xii, 3, 21, 52, 54, 65, 71, 72, 78, 104
response, 33, 92
reverse transcriptase, 79
rights, 71, 72, 81, 83
risk(s), x, xi, 1, 2, 4, 6, 8, 9, 10, 11, 12, 13, 14, 15, 16, 17, 19, 29, 31, 33, 36, 37, 39, 43, 45, 46, 67, 69, 70, 71, 73, 74, 75, 76, 77, 78, 79, 80, 82, 83, 84, 99, 104, 107
risk factors, x, 1, 2, 4, 6, 8, 9, 10, 11, 12, 13, 14, 15, 16, 17, 31, 45, 75, 104
risky behaviors,, xii, 81
roots, 24, 29

Royal Society, 48
rural population, 16, 76, 82
rural women, 21
Russia, 2
Rwanda, 44, 68

S

safety, ix, 73, 77, 90, 91, 100, 107
Samoa, 11
SAS, 4
Saudi Arabia, xi, 3, 10, 23, 24, 31, 32, 56, 58, 61, 62, 63
scaling, 87
scarcity, 52, 64, 66, 106
scholarship, ix
school, 70, 72, 75, 78, 86, 92, 94
schooling, 70, 84, 105
seafood, 24, 29
security, 66, 69, 70, 77
self-efficacy, 75
services, 15, 49, 50, 69, 71, 72, 77, 80
sewage, 94, 96, 104
sex, 46, 67, 73, 75, 76, 77, 78, 80, 82, 84, 91, 93, 97
sexual activity, 37, 75, 78
sexual behavior, 36, 75, 82
sexual contact, 45, 76
sexual health, 71
sexual violence, 67, 72
sexuality, xii, 76, 78, 81, 87
sexuality education, xii, 81
sexually transmitted diseases, 74, 83, 84, 99
sexually transmitted infections, 67, 75
shortage, 104
Siberia, 12
Sierra Leone, 44
Singapore, 87
social attitudes, 72
social development, 65
social interactions, 69
social network, 67, 77
social norms, 81
social roles, xiii, 99
social services, 70

social status, 30
social welfare, 69, 70
society, 78, 99
socioeconomic status, 21
Somalia, xi, 38, 43, 44, 57, 59, 62, 64
South Africa, 15, 75, 82, 83, 86, 87
South Korea, 13
Soviet Union, 44
Spain, 11, 12
speculation, 20
spending, 20
Spring, 106
Sri Lanka, 13, 18
stakeholders, 73, 80, 105
standard deviation, 23
standard error, 7, 54, 60, 61, 62
state(s), xiii, 11, 36, 40, 41, 42, 45, 49, 92
statistics, 25, 30, 47, 51, 54, 65
sterile, 46
stigma, 70, 71, 72, 75, 82
STIs, xii, 81
stress, 45, 70
stressors, 83
structural adjustment, 69, 71
structural characteristics, 70
structure, 84
style, x, 1, 9
sub-Saharan Africa, 70, 71, 74, 75, 84, 85
subsidy, 69
Sudan, xi, 12, 23, 24, 32, 37, 38, 41, 43, 44, 48, 57, 59, 62, 64, 100, 101, 102, 103, 104, 107
surveillance, 15, 39, 49, 72, 78, 90
survival, 22, 69
survivors, 77
Sustainable Development, 66
sweeteners, 24
Switzerland, 34
symbolism, 30
symptoms, 41
synthesis, x
syphilis, 42, 49
Syria, xi, 23, 24, 55, 56, 58, 61, 62

T

Taiwan, 11
Tajikistan, 32
Tanzania, 10, 82, 83, 84
target, 77
taxes, 25
techniques, 53, 65
technology(ies), 21
telephone, 45
temperature, xi, 51, 53, 54, 55, 58, 59, 60, 61, 62, 63, 65
territory, 103
testing, xii, 45, 71, 72, 74, 81
The Food and Agriculture Organization, x
therapy, 74, 75, 79, 82
thoughts, 69
threats, 66
time periods, 24, 28
Togo, 44
Tonga, 3, 11
total water requirements, xi, 107
tourism, 76
traditions, 1
training, 72, 80, 90
transmission, xi, 36, 37, 39, 43, 46, 47, 71, 73, 74, 75, 76, 79, 80, 81, 82, 83, 84, 85, 86, 87
transportation, 21, 45
treatment, xi, xii, 10, 20, 35, 39, 42, 46, 70, 71, 75, 76, 77, 78, 80, 81, 83, 84, 85, 86
trial, 81, 83, 86
triglycerides, 2
tuberculosis, 42, 48, 70, 82
Tunisia, xi, 23, 24, 57, 59, 61, 63, 101, 102, 103, 104, 107
Turkey, 16, 23, 33, 41, 47
type 2 diabetes, 11, 12, 13, 14, 16, 17, 18

U

ulcer, 76
UNDP, 53, 66
UNHCR, 37, 49

United Arab Emirates, xi, 3, 16, 23, 24, 33, 56, 58
United Kingdom (UK), 53, 66, 106
United Nations, x, 22, 25, 32, 34, 36, 49, 71, 85, 100, 107, 108
United Nations High Commissioner for Refugees, 49
United States, xi, 14, 37, 38, 39, 40, 42, 43, 44, 47, 48, 49, 90
urban, 10, 11, 12, 13, 14, 15, 16, 17, 18, 21, 31, 67, 76, 80, 83, 101, 103, 106
urban areas, 76
urban population, 10, 11, 12, 13, 14, 17, 18, 31, 67, 103
urbanisation, 17
urbanization, x, 10, 19, 20, 21, 33, 91
Uzbekistan, 14

V

vaccine, 45, 70, 86
Vanuatu, 17
variables, 29, 91, 97, 104
variations, 97
varimax rotation, 94
varimax rotation method, 94
vegetable oil, 24, 29
vegetables, 21, 24
vertical transmission, 42
victims, 20
Vietnam, 12, 44
violence, xii, 67, 80, 81, 86, 90, 107
viral infection, 41
virus infection, 47, 48
viruses, 45
vocabulary, 45
vulnerability, 54, 58, 61, 66, 69, 70, 83

W

Washington, 84, 106, 107
waste, 92, 94
waste disposal, 92
wasteful use of water resources, xii
water, ix, xi, xii, 51, 52, 53, 54, 55, 56, 57, 58, 60, 61, 62, 63, 64, 65, 66, 85, 89, 91, 92, 94, 96, 99, 103, 104, 106, 107
water quality, 104
water resources, xi, 52, 53, 56, 57, 65
wealth, 29, 30
web, 53, 106
weighted ranking score system, xii, 89, 93
welfare, 70
well-being, 70
West Africa, 47, 85, 87
withdrawal, 53, 56, 57, 58, 63, 64
workers, 46, 72, 76, 77, 80, 82, 84, 92
World Bank, 25, 34, 64, 66, 100, 102, 104, 108
World Health Organization (WHO), x, xii, 2, 4, 5, 8, 15, 18, 20, 22, 23, 33, 35, 36, 37, 40, 42, 49, 68, 83, 89, 91, 92, 100, 101, 102, 103, 104, 107, 108
World Trade Organization, 71
worldwide, x, 3, 7, 8, 20, 35, 36, 54, 91, 100

Y

Yemen, xi, 23, 24, 31, 56, 58, 59, 60, 62, 64
young people, 72, 78, 81, 86, 99
young women, 68, 76, 84
Yugoslavia, 44

Z

Zimbabwe, 68, 82